PATRICK KAVANAGH:

BY NIGHT UNSTARRED

PATRICK KAVANAGH

BY NIGHT UNSTARRED
An Autobiographical Novel

Edited by Peter Kavanagh

THE GOLDSMITH PRESS   THE CURRAGH   IRELAND

We acknowledge the help of An Chomhairle Ealaion
(The Arts Council)

Front Cover: Patrick Kavanagh, drawing by Brian Bourke.
Back Cover: Peter Kavanagh, drawing by Charles Cullen.

NH- 767678

ISBN 0.904984.26.5

Ireland 1977

Child, remember this high dunce
Had laughter in his heart and eyes,
A million echoes distance thence
Ere Dublin taught him to be wise.

UNLOADING THE HEART

When Patrick was growing up there was in progress a literary stirring called the Renaissance which was characterised largely by white-washed cottages, by peasants speaking a synthetic dialect and by the absence in writing of anything resembling thought. It was inevitable that Patrick would get a whiff of this sometimes fatal disease. Hence in 1938 his purported autobiography, **The Green Fool,** all the more unfortunate because it was well written.

It was a juvenile mistake he was not allowed to forget. In later years those who could not abide his prophetic message responded by praising **The Green Fool.**

Something had to be done about it and in 1950 I urged him to write his true autobiography. The idea appealed to him. If only he could find a form that would avoid the disastrous "I am". How also could he write of the women in his life and yet not identify them? He lacked the technique, he assured me, to express all that these women offered. At the same time he was inhibited by the knowledge that vanity about women is a bore. He had many other objections.

Nonetheless I urged him to make the attempt. It was important to record the struggle he had in Dublin and the genesis of those with whom he had to contend. He said he would do his best. He used the novel form—— for him a tired and tedious vehicle. He ended up with two novels, both incomplete. Many years later he was still interested in the idea and tried to make a distillation out of what he had written. I have taken up that challenge and the result will appear in the following pages. First a sketch of Patrick's early life.

Patrick Kavanagh born 21st October 1904 at forty-five minutes past eight on Sunday night in fine weather. Sponsors: John McCaffrey and Mary McCaffrey.
(From a Family Record Book)
The place of Patrick Kavanagh's birth was in the parish of Innis-

keen which is about mid-way between the towns of Dundalk and Carrickmacross. There is an Inniskeen village a mile distant from the family house but curiously this village was not part of his environment. As he himself explained later:

"...Oddly enough the village, though only a mile from my birth-place was always outside the orbit of my most intimate interests. To know fully even one field or one lane is a lifetime's experience. In the world of poetic experience it is depth that counts and not width.

A gap in a hedge, a smooth rock surfacing a narrow lane, a view of a woody meadow, the stream at the junction of four small fields — these are as much as a man can fully experience.

As I wander slowly along the overhanging hedge that separates my fields from the fields of John Woods my past life comes vividly alive in my imagination. Those wonderful days in a world that was only a couple of townlands and yet was eternal....

But sacred and profane literature has many examples to prove that a man's environment has little or nothing to do with his soul. This belief in the importance of environment and background is indeed one of the basic principles of Communism and to accept it is to accept something that is false and wicked. However, there is a way, out. If a thing is amusing or interesting and the idea is only accepted for its humorous implications, when personal dignity is not offended,then it is tolerable".

Since I was born twelve years later—— in March 1916—— I only know of Patrick's youth from hearsay. He went to school when he was four years old at nearby Kednaminsha and there under the stern discipline of Miss Cassidy he learned what are called the three Rs. He was a lazy student by all accounts but this lack of interest may have been the fault of his teacher. "My abiding memory of her", he wrote, "was the armful of canes she carried." "I don't believe in Solomon's theory of spare the rod and spoil the child. indeed, I know that any caning I received caused resentment in me towards the donor. My father, believed in the rod and I have never frogiven him. It isn't merely physical but mental injury that corporal punishment causes".

After "majoring" in kicking a rag ball he retired from formal schooling at the age of thirteen and devoted most of his time to roaming over the local lanes and fields. But his days at Kednaminsha were not entirely barren. The schoolbooks introduced him to poetry. "If I had roots." he wrote, "then they certainly were in the schoolbooks."

"For me when I read 'Eugene Aram' I am back in my native place, aged about sixteen with all my dreams sealed in the bud.

He told how murders walked the earth
Beneath the curse of Cain,
With crimson clouds before their eyes,
And flames about their brain,
For blood has left upon their soul
Its everlasting stain

"There am I walking down a lane peeping through the privet hedge into the field of turnips. The mood and atmosphere of the time comes alive in my mind. The comfortable worry of the summer fields is upon me. All the bits and pieces that furnish Imagination's house come up by magic. 'Locksley Hall' and I am several years younger.

"Even the covers of the schoolbooks add to the evocative impulse. **Eugene Aram** was in a bright yellow cover, **Locksley Hall** in a blue. They had a particular smell too.

Bret Harte's **Dickens in Camp** comes to mind:

Above the pines the moon was slowly drifting
The river sang below
The dim Sierras far beyond uplifting
Their minarets of snow.

"And that was me in the virginal time before I had ever thought of writing a verse. A strange time too— difficult to visualise for a man who afterwards became so deeply involved in verse. How strange a thing like that happens to a man. He dabbles in something and does not realise that it is his life. There is nothing deliberate or conscious about my beginnings. It all happened like an accident. When I read——

Often I think of the beautiful town
That is seated by the sea....

"I am walking through a field called Lurgankeel away down in a shady corner; it is an October evening and all around me is the protecting fog of family life. How shall I live when the fog is blown away and I am left alone naked?

"...But it is to the schoolbooks I must return for my virginal youth, for a winter morning in a desk near the fire, near the map of Scotland, with my head dipped in a new satchel sniffing the

9

wonderful memorable smell of new canvas."

Father was a shoemaker of the traditional kind—— he made new boots as well as repairing old ones. His "shop" formed part of the kitchen-living room. There he worked from early morning until nine at night. On leaving school Patrick was apprenticed to the trade. He was an indifferent learner but eventually made himself into a tolerable tradesmen. During those times of the year when a neighbouring farmer—— if you could call him that—— was especially busy with his crops, Patrick would leave the shoemaker's bench to lend a hand. In exchange for his work the neighbour would plant and harvest our family crop which we grew on land rented from the nearby Kenny estate.

The Dublin Insurrection of 1916 came and went without a ripple in our household or even in the district. The coming of the Black & Tans in 1920 caused a stir. Many of our neighbours were arrested and interned. Patrick was only sixteen at the time and was not lifted. Had he been he would eventually have ended up with a pension. Whether this would have changed the course of his life I cannot say.

Although Patrick had no political interests he drifted along with the wave of nationalism and began attending the Gaelic language class that started in the village and also joined the pipers band. He played the pipes adequately. After the "liberation" of 1922 and the subsequent Civil War our family continued as political observers and took no side.

In 1923 Patrick contracted typhoid fever which left him with a permanent thrombosis in one leg. This deformation did not however prevent him from extending his interest in sports to middle-distance running, the high jump, tug- o'war, and eventually goal-keeper for the local football team. This latter game as played in Inniskeen was a carry-over of the mediaeval battle. Legs, arms and jaws were occasionally broken and though Patrick's position was more or less stationary it carried a considerable risk. He survived serious injury, possible because of the family prayers that went with him each time he went into action.

I watched him play many times and I would rate him as well above average. He was of powerful build, had an excellent pair of hands, and was expert at kicking a dead ball. Once during a tournament he changed to the position of centre forward and within twenty minutes had scored six goals. The anger of the opposition at this feat as well as the envy of his team-mates forced him to retreat to the sidelines.

During the 1920s it became apparent that the days of the boot-maker were over, so our family decided to diversify by buying a small farm half a mile from our house—— called Reynold's farm. It consisted of seven small watery fields facing north. To help to cultivate this new property we also invested in a secondhand cart and an old mare that was ready for the knackers. A neighbour called Mat Rooney had only one horse and by joining forces with him we now had a team. The plough Patrick used was the primitive sort that didn't even have a wheel to guide its depth. It was while guiding this plough that Patrick wrote:

I turn the lea-green down
Gaily now
And paint the meadow brown
With my plough.

The joint enterprise of Patrick and Mat Rooney created great comment and even merriment in the district.

Some of Patrick's happiest days, and mine too, were spent sitting on the hills of Reynold's farm and looking north towards Glassdrummond chapel and the Mourne mountains.

Inniskeen and its environs even in the twenties continued to be a part of mediaeval Ireland. The "Talkies" were still to be invented and Television was long in the future. The local entertainment, when work was done, was to gather at the crossroad for conversation or pitch-halfpenny. Sometimes there might be a gathering of forty or more on a bright summer evening. Storytelling in the homes was also very common—— stories of ghosts, fairies, evil spirits and the rest. There was a strong tradition here. This was Carleton country. A mile or two away, near where my mother was born, was The Wild Goose lodge. I had heard the story orally long before I had read Carelton's version.

Card parties were very common—— the games of Nap, Fifteen and Eucre—— and Patrick participated eagerly.

Now and then dances were held in someone's loft to celebrate some special event. Patrick attended but was awkward and shy with the neighbouring girls. I don't blame him a bit—— they were socially uncouth and wouldn't mind wounding a man's sensibilities. They might be interested but they were inclined to cover up their eagerness with a coarse bravado. There was no point in risking one's ego.

A somewhat less formal event was the "stir". It was held in the house with fewer people invited. Patrick described such an event:

THE STIR

"Why aren't you going down to the stir?" the son of the house said to me in a grumbling voice.

I was sitting in the kitchen listening to an old man telling old stories. I wasn't pulling my weight. After all, the stir had been organised for the young people, and for me to stay sitting in the kitchen listening to the old people wasn't very courteous. The stir was being held in the Big Room behind the fireplace. In the Little Room on the other side of the kitchen (it was a one-storey, three-roomed house) the tea, or supper if you like, was being served. It was from the Big Room - and those taking part in the stir - that people were being called in rotation to supper, so I reluctantly left my old storytelling friend and, stooping my head (I was always big for my age) to avoid striking it on the low lintel of the Big Room door, I joined the merrymakers at the stir.

The stir was what they called a private dance.

The dancers were seated around the walls on the sideboards of carts which rested on bags of meal, the girls mostly on men's knees.

A noted entertainer from the town of Louth was present and had just concluded a song. The jazz age was beginning and it was a jazzy type of song; I thought it marvellous. He was about to begin another song but the son of the house who was M.C. was about fed-up with him. It took him the best part of an hour's forcing to get the singer started and now it was almost as hard to get him to stop once he had got warmed up.

"Take your partners for a one-shtep".

But the man from the town of Louth was off again, to my great delight. The majority of those present were out of sympathy with this new type of song; even so, through force of habit the end of each verse received the traditional encouragement of "Rise it, ye boy ye!" and "Good on ye!"

It was a summer's night. The harsh call of the corncrake kept up a continuous rhythmic beat. From the horse's stable came an unusual noise. Was the horse caught in the manger? The son of the house glared at the man from Louth as much as saying that he had frightened the horse. He rushed out but returned shortly saying "Nothing wrong".

The eight people who had been having supper in the Little Room filed back into the Big Room. The daughter of the house tapped eight other people on the shoulder with the words, "Go on down now". She passed me by and I felt wounded; this was a real test of how well you were thought of. I was almost a next-door neighbour but it showed how little was thought of you when it came to the whipping of crutches. And there wasn't more than two more lots to be served. I would probably be left to the last, and so it happened. But I was grateful for all that; after all, I had been invited.

The Little Room was very little. A table had been placed lengthwise along two beds. Four of us sat on the edge of the bed and the other four jammed against the wall on the other side.

There was bags of bread and jam: it was a great feast and we all felt inclined to gaiety.

I was a bit uneasy; I seemed to be under suspicion. A second daughter of the house who was in charge of this department had what I was later to discover were all the attributes of the owner of a lounge bar. She had a stern and nasty attitude that would stand no unconventional nonsense. That terrible fear of the unconventional is a queer thing. Most people have something to conceal and the unconventional is always likely to bare the secret. I had merely stretched myself for a moment back on the bed.

Shortly afterwards the M.C. looked in the low door and stared at me. I never ate a male's mate that did me less good. Gingerly I stabbed with my knife for the slices of bread. I put on the jam with trembling hands. I did everything gently.

Next thing was, didn't the leg of the bed on my side give and we were all on the ground with the cups of tea held—— if we were lucky—— poised above our foreheads. We managed to get to our feet. It transpired that the leg of the bed was a sack of oats that had slipped sideways. I eventually extricated myself from an awkward situation and the rest of the supper passed pleasantly.

I remember that Little Room well. On the damp walls hung all the usual holy pictures that were to be found in a small country house. On the mantleboard over a rusty fireplace stood a faded photograph of a wedding with the bridegroom wearing side-whiskers. Grandfather of the M.C.

"It's a bleddy good stir", I said.

"Make a dousing wake", said the fellow opposite me when the daughter of the house had gone for more tea.

We were not conscious of any element of pathos though the material was there. Pleasure is comparative.

When everyone had supper the stir got going in earnest. The fiddler played and left as few gaps as possible through which the man from the town of Louth could enter with another of his jazzy songs. I protested loudly that I thought the man from Louth damn good. Then the M.C. said: "How about yourself giving us a stave?"

"I would only I can't think of the words of any song", I said.

There was silence. I tried to think but no song came to my memory. Just as the silence was being broken by jeering banter I recalled the words of "McKenna's Dream".

> *One night of late I chanced to stray*
> *It being in the pleasant month of May*
> *While all the green in slumber lay*
> *The moon sank in the deep.*

Sang it right through in spite of interruptions. And as God is my judge when I was finished I tossed my head from side to side and said what a million singers had said before without knowing that anyone had ever said it before—— "A good song but a very hard song to sing".

Patrick and I had seven sisters who gradually drifted off into the nursing profession. While at home they treated Patrick with considerable familiarity and lack of respect. Patrick was able to reply in kind but it should not have been necessary. Mother, however, took no such attitude and regarded him as the favourite.

I first became aware of Patrick when I was about seven or eight years old. When he came home from work in the fields, no matter how tired he was, he would play with me in the Front Garden either kicking a rag ball or merely playing tag. That memory remained with both of us, and when he was about to enter hospital with cancer in 1955 he wrote a verse to be inserted in **The Prelude** dedicated to that experience:

14

Remember well your noble brother
Whose constant heart embraced no other
But you, and when love's arteries harden
Evoke the image of the Front Garden,
Yellow with sunlit weeds, and there
You are the hound and he the hare,
And round and round you run and laugh.
This moment is immortal stuff.
Name his name, beloved name Peter
And only regret that words must fail
To tell that marvellous brotherly tale.

By the time I came to know Patrick he had been writing verse for a number of years:

The poplars grow in splendor there
The fields are white as snow
With posies bright and proud and fair
Their beauties are beyond compare
When they bend their tresses to and fro
In March when stormy winds do blow.

Gradually I became Patrick's audience for everything he wrote and so it remained up to the time of his death.

By the time Patrick began writing, the local Bard of Callenberg was retiring from verse. He was a man with a wicked tongue and was ready to use it in rhyme on the slightest provocation. Patrick recalls:

"Around about twelve or so I took to the poeming, as it is called. Quite a lot of terror filled the hearts of my parents when they heard the news. Was he going to be another Bard?"

While members of his family and neighbours were cogitating on this awful possibility Patrick suddenly went public. He submitted verse to a poetry competition in the **Weekly Irish Independent** in August 1928. Three were accepted. It was a dramatic, a memorable moment in both our lives. Patrick writes:

"I have only felt excitement three times in regards to my work. The first of these was one morning when I was pulling the chaff from a mill at a threshing my brother, who was a schoolboy at the time, came running up to bring me a letter from the **Weekly Independent** which, when I opened it, read: 'The Editor was accepting three poems of mine—— 'Summer', 'The Pessimist', and 'Freedom'.

The second was when I got a letter from AE (George Russell) saying that he liked the poems I sent him but couldn't use them and would I send him some more; and the third was when I received a small blue envelope from **The Spectator** saying that the then Literary Editor (Peter Fleming) was keeping three poems for publication".

My family was embarrassed and our neighbours shocked at Patrick's brashness in writing for a newspaper. Patrick didn't remain long with the **Weekly Independent** and as far as the neighbours knew he had given up writing. Patrick discovered AE and his **Irish Statesman**. Up to this time Patrick had no means of travelling except on foot or by train. Then Jemmy Quinn, an uncle crippled with arthritis, gave Patrick his old bicycle. Now Patrick was able to travel at will to Dundalk and it is here he came across the **Irish Statesman**. His first verse "The Intangible" was published there 19th October 1929, and on the 15th February of the following year, "Ploughman".

1929 was an eventful year. Patrick was launched on a literary career. It was also the year of father's death, making Patrick nominal head of the household—— though mother held the reins. It was also the year the decision was made to send me to High School with a view to my becoming a National Teacher. My sister Lucy already had achieved that distinction and with her help and help from the rest of my sisters it was thought possible to pay my expenses. So it was that beginning in 1929 I started cycling the six miles to Carrickmacross High School every day except Sunday. I wasn't especially bright but I had stamina and determination —— determination that I was going to succeed and with my success would be success for Patrick. I realised he was special and no ordinary versifier. He didn't belong in Inniskeen.

While I was studying my schoolbooks Patrick did not rest on a headland waiting for me to rescue him. In 1930 and the following two years he made several pilgrimages to Dublin to introduce himself to the literary world. In retrospect it is embarrassing to think of it. There was no literary world in Dublin. He himself was the literary world and didn't know it. Neither did I. In the course of one such trip AE (George Russell) gave Patrick a load of books. Two of those books were important to him, **Gil Blas** and **Moby Dick**. He read and re-read them up to the time of his death. I read all the others: Plato, the Russians, Victor Hugo, Frank O'Connor and several others.

He also began to send out selections of his verse to various English publishers. Eventually Macmillans accepted and in 1936 published his first book **Ploughman & Other Poems**. It was widely reviewed because of who published it but no one around Inniskeen as far as I know bought a copy. It would have been a good investment today as it is now rare. The verse in this slim volume was thin and yet one piece "Inniskeen Road" has achieved a certain popularity.

A road, a mile of kingdom, I am king
Of banks and stones and every blooming thing.

A worthless kingdom, was Patrick's comment on it later on.

In 1936 I could scarcely believe my good fortune—— I graduated as a National Teacher from St. Patrick's Training College, Dublin. Now I had a profession, a respectable profession, and all I needed was to find a job and start earning money to support Patrick as well as myself—— or at the very least give Patrick a start. Jobs were hard to come by in those days but I got a temporary one teaching in the De La Salle School in Dundalk at forty-seven and threepence a week. I was in the money!

At once I began urging Patrick to try his luck in London. I would be at home to take care of mother and the watery fields. He was persuaded largely because I tyrannised over him. He really loved his little fields. I assured him I would take good care of everything and so off he went; a few extra shillings in his pocket to make his name in London.

He put up at Rowton House, a ninepence a night shelter and began his assault on London. Helen Waddell had been the reader for Macmillans who recommended publication of his book of verse. He called on her. She recommended him to Constables who in turn asked him to write his autobiography. He moved from Rowton house to the apartment of John Gawsworth, an anthologist who had been writing to him. Gawsworth put him up for a month or more while he worked on **The Green Fool**. He searched in vain for work that would give him a living. He failed, and soon returned to Inniskeen. There he finished **The Green Fool**.

The Green Fool was turned down by Constable. They recommended it to Michael Joseph, then starting up as a publisher. He accepted it and begged Sean O'Casey to write an introduction. O'Casey refused on the grounds that introductions are useless. He also suggested to Patrick that he should "tread down the grapes."

Immediately on publication Oliver Gogarty sued for libel. He had been mentioned innocently enough in the book. Michael Joseph settled without contest and the book was dead.

To the surprise of everyone as well as myself I turned out to be a terrific teacher, to such a degree that at the end of my first year I was rated Highly Efficient by the Department of Education inspector. Dublin needed teachers with this rating to retain their special accreditation so without any trouble I got a job teaching in the Christian Brothers School, Westland Row. The year was 1937.

I continued to urge Patrick to leave Inniskeen. He was unhappy with the lack of respect he received there and also complained that hard manual labour was bad for the mind. Once more he tried his luck in London hoping to get literary work reviewing books and such like. The irrationality of this hope came home to me with a vengeance only recently when I read Harold Nicholson's **Diaries** of the period. Fellows like Nicholson with top connections were crowding each other out for these jobs. What chance had Patrick? So he came back to Ireland and settled in with me in Dublin, first in a bedsitter on Upper Drumcondra Road and after that in another bedsitter at 35 Haddington Road. The year was 1939 and from this year on Patrick was a permanent resident of Dublin. Mother was still alive and Patrick went down frequently to Inniskeen to visit her but practically his home was now in Dublin.

The sentimental tone of **The Green Fool** and the slight **Ploughman** verses made Patrick eminently eligible for the AE Memorial Award of one hundred pounds. Those who gave the prize were unaware at the time of his massive integrity. They soon learned and that was to be the last prize he ever got from an Irish source.

Dublin was infinitely more malicious than London but it was smaller and, it was thought, more easy to conquer. Patrick set about that task with a will. Twenty years later he was still at it and still starving. He recalls:

"The Hitler war was started. I have no job, no real friends. I live by writing articles for the papers mainly on the pleasures of country life which, fifty miles away, calls me to return. There is a new prosperity owing to the war but I, a mad messiah without a mission or a true impulse, struggle on in Dublin instead of walking out...

For many years after my misfortunate arrival in the City devoted

18

to The Lie I was terribly concerned about things Irish and I slashed out all round me. My misfortune——apart from that flaw of character which must be the original Original Sin——was that I grew up in a society which was locked in a literary idea that was purely English and which called itself The Irish Literary Revival. This literary jag cut a man off not just from Europe but from the spiritual realities of things seen and loved".

I was earning eleven pounds a month. Out of this I paid twelve shillings rent per week for the bedsitter and the rest was devoted to food, clothes and luxuries. I had to be at school at nine. Patrick would spend the morning writing and then join me for lunch in an underground restaurant near the school where the food consisted mainly of potatoes. But what beautiful potatoes—— large and floury. After lunch meet again at six, have tea and spend the rest of the evening in diversion, To bed at ten-thirty. Always.

After a year we moved to a somewhat larger bedsitter at 122 Morehampton Road. The rent was fourteen shillings a week but the cooker was outside under the stairs. We had to share it with the landlady. It was at this address Patrick wrote "The Great Hunger" —— in longhand since neither of us owned a typewriter. From there we moved to a flat over a cinema near O'Connell Bridge. We stayed only a few months but long enough for Patrick to complete his long poem "Lough Derg". Finally we ended up in a large unfurnished flat at 62 Pembroke Road. This flat remained for the most part unfurnished until the day we left many years later. We could not afford to furnish it. Here **Tarry Flynn** and a great part of his writings first saw the light.

It soon became apparent that I would have to advance to a better job if I were to continue to support Patrick. With this in mind I started evening courses at UCD and by 1941 I had collected the M.A. Through the good offices of W.B. Stanford I was invited to do a Ph.D. at Trinity College and towards the end of December 1944 I graduated. Patrick was delighted with my achievement. No longer would I be tied to Ireland. I could move and perhaps he could follow. Mother died in 1945 and the following year I left for America.

Patrick stormed every barricade of church, of state and of high society in his search for a living but was always rebuffed. Here is a sample from Sean McEntee, Minister for Industry & Commerce dated 9th August 1940:

"Further to the acknowledgement of the contents of your letter of the 24th ultimo addressed to Mrs. McEntee...I should perhaps explain that in general all posts in the Government service, particularly those requiring clerical qualifications are filled competitively through the Civil Service Commission. On occasions when very special circumstances warrant it the Departments are authorised to recruit temporary staff through the Labour Exchange. These occasions are very few and far between but before any candidate can be considered for a vacancy so arising it is an essential rule that he must be registered as unemployed at the Labour Exchange..."

Patrick even sought a job as freelance lecturer in schools and it was while delivering some such lecture at Blackrock College that he first met the future Archbishop of Dublin, John Charles McQuaid. Patrick sought patronage from the archbishop but received only charity. Still——. Another bishop, this one from the west of Ireland, persuaded Peter Curry, Editor of **The Standard**, to put Patrick on as sub-editor and film critic. It was the only job he ever got.

"Dublin! Have I ever belonged there?" wrote Patrick some years later. "I find it hard to use the word 'Dublin' with confidence. It makes me somewhat ashamed. A place has no value in isolation from our faith in it."

But though Patrick ended up having no faith in Dublin we who are recording his environment must suspend judgment and let the novel we have promised state the position. First we must set the scene.

SCENE

The year is 1941. It is a Sunday evening and Patrick is walking down a Dublin street, Baggot Street, let us say. He has not a penny in his pocket—— his usual condition. But this evening he felt the lack of money more than ever for he had just seen passing in a racing car a girl he had recently been in love with. She was in the company of one of the young De Vines. Truth to tell, Patrick was still in love with her even though in the meantime he had become deeply attached to another young girl. Patrick's capacity for love was intense. This evening Margaret was studying for her university examinations and could not be with him. That's what she told him.

Then I went to the heath and the wild,
To the thistles and thorns of the waste,
And they told me how they were beguiled,
Driven out and compelled to be chaste.

He tried to console himself with Blake's lines. He was compelled to be chaste. He would be satisfied now with a cigarette. He couldn't stop a stranger on the street and ask for a cigarette; his pride would not let him. So he walked on thinking angry thoughts. He wouldn't have minded so much his penniless condition if the uncle of that young scamp who had taken his girl hadn't gone out of his way to blacken his name charging him with being the enemy of faith and morals just when he had the chance of getting a job.

The De Vines were tremendously important in the city of Dublin, in the whole country, in fact. Henry, father of the fellow in the car was one of the country's biggest businessmen. He was also interested in art and music. Henry gave gramophone concerts and had a fine collection of modern paintings. Patrick had the chance once of becoming acquainted with this man. That he did not do so was because he had got a casual job writing about an art show of Henry's favourite painter. Patrick had written what he thought fair criticism yet the man was venomously angry. For a lover of art there was something bitter and cruel about Henry De Vine.

Henry's sister had a reputation as a concert pianist and once more Patrick made some adverse criticism. He sensed something vulgar and frightening in her mind.

Another brother was a Capuchin priest who was reputed to be one of the saintliest men and one of the most ascetic in the country. He had immense power among big businessmen.

As he walked disconsolately along the street that evening Patrick met an actor.

"Are you coming to Mrs. De Vine's At Home?" the actor asked.

"I'd hate to and, besides, I wasn't invited."

"Ah, come on. I know them well", said the actor.

Patrick knew this to be true. The De Vines were warm admirers of actors and actresses. He hesitated awhile but finally gave in. At least he would get cigarettes at the party and he might be able to work his way into the regard of Father Joseph.

His arrival at the party caused something of a shock. As he

21

entered the crowded drawingroom all eyes stared at him making him very self-conscious.

The old father, a man of near eighty, sat in an armchair in the corner talking to a visiting jockey about racehorses. There was a dribble of senile saliva from his mouth. He picked his nose.

The discussion going on was all about the latest play or rather, about the actors who played in it.

Patrick tried to make conversation with a neighbour but she soon turned away from him to talk to an actor. After some time the Capuchin arrived and found a seat beside Patrick. What a lucky chance this would be, Patrick thought! He drew around the subject of a job he had in mind but the priest suddenly changed his tune.

"That last thing you wrote was atrocious." he snarled. "How dare you come to ask me for a favour? You are one of those blackguards, enemies of faith and morals."

Good and Evil. That great mystery forces its way into our story.

We are now compelled to leave waiting to oneside, the story of Patrick as he continues his pilgrimage around Dublin in order that we may examine with some minuteness the genesis of that evil he is encountering.

CHAPTER 1

The Fall of Human Nature surely did not happen in Time and Space. Whatever happens one second before a man's birth into this world has for him an antiquity more remore than the oldest saga story. The moment of a man's conception is the closing against him of the Gates of Eden.

Peter De Vine—— he who was over there in the armchair picking his nose and talking to the jockey—— was thrown out of the Garden of Eden into the parish of Ballyrush in the year 1867. It was a hilly district with an interest in the three counties of Monaghan, Louth and Armagh, about six miles west of the sea-port of Dundalk.

It was a parish of small farms, not that either the location or the source of livelihood are of the highest importance, for life is the same everywhere. Yet the poverty of the place, the shape of the hills and the twist of the roads did give a certain individual colour to the thoughts of the people.

The average farm was between six and nine acres. Peter's father had twelve and this fact made him a somewhat stubborn, proud man. He kept a good horse all the year round while his neighbours were usually engaged in sampling varieties of viciousness in crooked steeds. A kicker replaced a biter, the wind-broken replaced by a wind-sucker. Having been so long forced to live in the company of such notorious horse traders the people of this place were generally dreaded at home and abroad.

Peter's father was too respectable to become a horse-huckster and, as a consequence, and in spite of his larger portion of land, he was poorer both spiritually and temporally than most of his immediate neighbours. Nearly all the lovely experiences of life are theirs who stand on the lower ledges of existence, a little dissolute. Poetry, romance, the magic of sunlight, the laugh in the fields, are not found dressed in solemn ritual.

Peter's father was a stern upright Christian and yet he was not a man that one could like. If a neighbour's goat trespassed into his cabbage garden he did not take it —— as the rest of the people took such a common occurrence —— as part of the game, abusing the owner of the offending goat and reading his seven generations inside and out. Peter's father would not act that way. He would drive a graip or hay fork in the goat and did so on more than one occasion. He had an unmusical whistle which, when his immediate neighbours heard it, filled them with the most unnatural terror.

He had four sons and one daughter though the daughter might be described as a son too, so masculine, so like her brothers was she. The daughter was the youngest, Peter the third youngest. The family with the exception of Peter were big and raw-boned and of low mentality. Peter too was of low mentality but he was small and slightly built with a thin face like a weasel.

As Peter was the only member of the family who did not vanish into the oblivion of the unwritten word he alone exists now in this other-world of the story.

So by the grace of God let him be revealed as a man, as a symbol of a new society, as a mirror for history.

Peter had received some education from the village teacher, a savage old man who was fond of the bottle. At the age of twelve he left school to join the tribe of semiserfs, the farm labourers. Those of the tribe with ambition dreamt of America, but even their wildest ambition was overwhelmed by the little fields. Like prisoners long in jail they had fallen in love with those fields and the last thing they wanted was liberation.

The acre field was a wide expanse, limitless in their imagination. A new field added to a farm was for the possessor a new world discovery. At the going away of a man for America there would be crying and lamentation by the sides of the roads and tears fell on the potatoes that were being weeded. And there were songs:

And when they'll return to the land of their birth,
They'll have no one to welcome them home.

It was terrible.

Peter Devine (for that was his real name) did not want to go to America. As he wrought in the fields of his uncle he sometimes daydreamed that his uncle might die and leave him the place. But he knew that was hopeless —— the uncle had a younger sister. Then he dreamed of Maggy Stanley and her lovely big field —— a big acre not counting the two gardens. He was no more than sixteen when he might be overheard daydreaming to himself: She's as good as new still, Maggy is—— eh?"

Then at the age of twenty he fell in love with the miller's daughter. He convinced himself that only his poverty, his dirty, coarse, farm clothes, and not his miserable appearance—— prevented him having her. All that summer season in the fields the storms of a useless passion swept across his heart.

He wanted to rest his heart and mind on something soft—— he wanted sympathy or he would go mad. He tried to daydream his old love of the land into his thoughts—— the soft sensuality of clay about his burning brain. He could not do it.

A year passed. His passion had passed too. Perhaps not passed but became something else. His power to love became a power for hate. His was the bitterness of a poet to whom God gave no talent.

He left his uncle to become a small dealer. He went to the fairs, bought and sold drop calves, young pigs, anything that there was a penny to be made in. In the intervals between fairs he practised pig-gelding, pig butchering and many other of the uncertain professions of the tillage country. He joined the Land League and every Sunday after second Mass in Ballyrush he sat in the village school where the old politicians talked of Davitt and Dillon and Blood Balfour.

As he listened to their speeches he realised that there were three facets of life upon which he could work and not be thwarted—— politics, land and religion. He did not like religion in that it meant praying; but there was another aspect of religion.

Men who are failures in the central passion of life, men without talent, can become great politicians, great businessmen or great churchmen. For two years he was lost in politics.

Coming home from a political meeting one September evening, deeply involved in conversation with another great politician, Tom Duffy, the postman, he unwittingly betrayed his frustrations.

"I'll tell you one thing you ought to remember," said the postman, "A man should never be afraid of doing damage to a girl. That is the way of the world and if you don't do it you will go down and stay down."

Peter was listening. He assumed a certain malice in the advice but he also saw truth in it. It may have been to some extent this advice that gave him courage in his ruthless dealing with Rosie Malone, the half-wit. But in the first instance it was his own natural

27

impulses that drew him towards her and away from his romantic love for the miller's daughter.

Rosie Malone was three months pregnant before her mother discovered it and without saying a word mother and daughter in the month of January made their way to the house of the Devines.

Mrs. Devine asked them in but they refused. Then the long-nosed thirty-year old daughter of the Devines, sensing something odd in the wind, came to the door to join in the discussion.

"Arra, what?" Mrs. Devine shouted, rising in a moment from calmness to the height of infuriated neighbourly hate. "God damn and double damn your sowls into hell and out of it". Then the daughter joined in. "Leave this place you bad characters. To think yous would have the assurance to come to try to blacken that brother of mine that wouldn't hurt a fly. Sure yous were always a dirty crowd, the whole rick-ma-tick of yous, big and small...."

The tirade could be heard across the townland. Mary Kerley pulling oaten straw from the stack for her cows heard it and cocked her ear. Maggy Stanley milking her goat heard.

Mrs. Malone and her daughter tried to answer in whispers. They tried too to escape but the relentless anger of the other women pursued them down the lane.

None of the men folk of the Devines appeared. Peter, who had been scraping turnips for the cow suspended the scraping knife's operation in the middle of the act. He held his breath.

The Malones went to the priest who then called on the Devines. The whole family put on their faces of righteousness, as they were so well able to do, and tried to give the priest the impression that a more wronged family wasn't in the parish.

A few days later Peter Devine left the country.

CHAPTER 2

"Would it be him?" cried Maggy Stanley.

"It's very like him", drawled her daughter Brigid.

Both Maggy Stanley and her daughter were standing on the sunny height on the heap of mortar at the gable of their whitewashed cottage straining their eyes to get a better view of the man with the travelling bag who was trying to beat his way through the hedge in Dooley's field where the stile used to be.

"It's either him or some stranger." said Maggy.

"No stranger would try to thrash down a gap," said Brigid.

"That's the truth, Brigid," agreed the mother. "Run in and bring us out the can till I run down to the well to get a better look at the low blackguard."

She grabbed the tin can and raced down the slope to the well which stood on the side of the road near the crossroads. As she ran, the excitement of being first with the news, if news it was, trembled in every part of her female body.

Standing on the flagged roof of the well and holding a briar aside that blocked the view, she could see the man clearly.

Crash, crash, crash! He had picked up a heavy piece of stick and was bringing it down on the barbed wire and thorny bushes that the Dooleys had placed across the right-of-way. Without a doubt it was Peter Devine. He was as ugly as ever. His face was yellow as a Chinaman's and his neck had as much loose skin as would go around it several times. Generations of bad living seemed to be looking out of his small streaky blue eyes. Although he was only thirty-four on the fifteenth of the previous month of July he looked anything from fifty upwards. He was like a thing that had never been young or innocent—— like an old goat.

Crash, crash, crash! Now he dropped the heavy stick and was cutting the barbed wire by chopping at it with two field stones—— one as an anvil, the other as a hammer.

When the Dooleys see this they will raise the right big row, thought Maggy.

He succeeded in cutting the wires and levelling the top of the bushes. He then flung his bag through the gap, took a short run at the gap and was out in the rich green corner of the adjoining field, briars and thorns trailing from his coat. He glanced back once at the gap he had made as if viciously saying to himself "By God, that's only the beginning of it. Anyone that blocks that right-o'-way again will have to deal with me."

Maggy was delighted, the terrified delight of a woman in the presence of a dangerous man. She stooped to fill her can at the well as Peter went on his way towards the gate that let onto the lane on the shoemaker Conlon's side of the crossroads. She thought he hadn't seen her, but she wouldn't trust him. He would pretend not to see if it didn't pay him. "By the holy smokes the Dooleys will come to their milk now," said Maggy to herself.

The Dooleys owned all the land around the Carrolls five-acre farm, and for people who were so straight and outwardly respectable, neither borrowing nor lending, they were not pleasant neighbours. They weren't quite normal, considered nothing but their own business and kept to themselves like ruthless morality, an unbending bar in the backbone of the townland of Ballyrush.

Maggy let the water splash over the sides of the can till half of it was spilled, so great was her hurry up the hill to tell her daughter the news.

"Oh it's him alright, back with us again like the bad weather", she told her daughter.

They both stood on the threshold of their door keeping their eyes on the figure of Peter Devine as he sidled up the lane past the shoemaker Conlon's.

"It's six years last April since he left," said Maggy, and by the looks of him he's home now with the same hole in his arse. Coming back like the rest of them to live on the clippings of tin."

"He'd be in a bad way if he weren't as good as the ould scraidins around here, Ma."

"Must have walked out on the black woman the postman says he married in England."

"You know well, Ma, he wouldn't marry a black woman. That's just the postman's auld lies. He's always at it."

"Well, right or wrong, the country was well rid of him but now that he's back there's one thing sure. I'll have a dry foot under me

30

this winter. I'll not have to go around the guttery lane, up to me knees in wet, now that the pad is sure to be open again. God! Peter is the boy who will make the Dooleys hop."

The boggy, whinny, stony townland through which Peter Devine walked with knowing feet and with sharp eye was one of those dark and remote districts where in those years of 1901 nothing had changed for a thousand years. It lay off the notorious road,

"From Carrickmacross to Crossmaglen
Where
There are more rogues than honest men."

Twenty or thirty years before there were highwaymen prowling that road —— or so it was related. Every man who had a penny to his name was believed to have inherited it from some ancestor who had robbed the mail coach. That was how the Dooleys got their cash, it was said by all the poorer people. At this time there were no highwaymen prowling along that mysterious tree-lined, hill-hung road, but there were scores of dealing men of all kinds —— notably the horse-dealers.

The main lane came straggling around the hill, taking more than a mile-and-a-half to cover a distance that by the short-cut across Dooley's fields would be no more than half a mile. And such a lane! humps and hollows and sudden rises—— and even in the middle of summer, parts of it were muddy and a foot deep in cow-dung since Dooley's cattle found shelter here from the flies in summer. The worst part of the lane was that which bordered the Dooley farm. And they wouldn't allow one inch to be taken off the sides so that it could be made a country road.

On the side of this lane lived the shoemaker Barney Conlon, and on the side of the hill beyond the shoemaker's house was the Devine's.

Peter's old white-haired mother—— as good a sample of Mother Macree as you would wish to see, was out feeding the turkeys on the hill before the door when she sighted her son returning. She dropped the bucket, rubbed her hands in the grass and rushed down the hill to greet him.

"Oh, thanks be to God, you're back, Peter, dear and darling," she cried.

She threw her arms around him. "Why the devil didn't you write and tell me you were coming so I could send one of these lazy good-for-nothing brothers of yours to meet you at the station and carry your bag? Give me the bag, here, and let me carry it."

He let her carry the bag.

"Oh, you're welcome as the flowers of May, Peter. No one could tell you the suffering I went through with these lazy loorpauns since you left. Look at them now watching you, and not one of them has the goodness to come down and say you're welcome back. Oh, but it's me who's glad you're back."

Two of the other three sons were busy that evening building a wall around the haggard. The third one was fixing a one-horse reaping machine which he had bought.

The house had been newly painted and all the farm implements in the yard were painted blue and red. The yard had been levelled and new stables built.

The mother flustered around the returned son, helping him off with his coat, asking him if he was tired and if he might like to lie down in her bed while she was preparing something for him to eat. Peter had always been his mother's pet. She was never done praising him at the expense of the other sons. Meeting the shoemaker's wife or Maggy Stanley she was sure to draw round the conversation to the good son. "If I was talking till tomorrow evening I wouldn't be able to tell you the good-goodness of that child", the shoemaker was in the habit of mimicking her.

Peter drank, and in drink it was hard to say if he was a mad man or a bad man. He had fought many fights both when drunk and when sober but no man who knocked him down or injured him might have a guilty conscience afterwards. For Peter was the falsest of fighters. In fairs any excuse to break a man's skull was a good excuse.

The three other sons were what is called "dacent unmeddling boys". They neither drank nor went with women, and better or tidier men around a farm it would be hard to find. The rick of corn built by Hughie who was the eldest, would take no hurt if it were left unthreshed for two years. Tom, the second eldest was one of the best scythemen in the country. He could knock an acre of corn in a day if there was any sort of lie on it. Pat, the youngest, was noted as one of the finest men ever to follow a pair of horses in a plough. And of course they were all famous for their skill as quarrymen. It was worth getting these men to make a face on a quarry. And to watch them handle the crow bar!

When as sometimes happened Peter had a broken head or was recovering from a bout of drinking, two of the other sons would be sent to the fair to sell cattle or pigs as the case might be. They would go and sell—— and sell well—— for they were good market-men—— and come home without as much as taking a cup of tea or a bun, not to mention going into a public house. Whatever they got for the beasts was brought home a prisoner and handed over to the mother. Then when they had handed over every penny they would begin to badger the woman for a couple of shillings for tobacco or for a football match.

"Well, yous are as mane a pair of men as ever walked behind a bullock; yous sell a baste and want all the money. It's me that's sorry that good child, Peter, wasn't fit to go out."

"And we never spent as much as a penny!"

The mother turned away in disgust. The sons went down the road to the village where penniless they hung around the lighted windows of the shops.

"Are yous not going to stand?" some of the horse dealers who knew Peter would say with a jeer.

Only too willing to stand drinks they were if they had any money, for they were as generous about standing as many tee-totallers are. As a result of all this they got the name of being mean while Peter with all his faults was considered a "damn sight straighter and dacenter man."

Now on the otherhand, when Peter went to the fair with cattle he usually put a couple of pounds in his pocket, got drunk on the loose change and came home to his mother in the middle of the night roaring like a madman and reading the seven generations of his next-door neighbours as he came up the lane or across by the cross-cut. The mother, who would be in bed would rise and cook him a meal of bacon and eggs. And if it happened to be winter she would have a hot-water bottle in the bed for him. While the mother would be cooking for him Peter would put a small bottle of whiskey on the table and say in a whisper, "Just a wee drop for yourself, Ma".

Ma would almost break down with emotion at this proof of her son's love, even though she herself never touched intoxicating liquor. Later on Peter would slip the bottle back in his pocket and put it under his pillow for his morning cure. When he went to bed the mother would tuck him in and generally pull the bed-clothes off the other son to make Peter snug.

Peter wasn't drunk, she told herself and everyone else. Peter never tasted a drop of drink in his life. It was just that he was high-tempered, the high temper that one always found in decent fellows, she said. Did anyone ever meet a good man that wasn't a bit fiery?

So now he was home again with her and she hoped he would never leave.

Hughie came in to light his pipe at the fire.

"Mind you don't let them dirty ashes fall on the pan" screamed the mother.

"You're back." said Hughie to his brother.

Peter gave a squealing reply, one of those frightened and frightening squeals which come up from some hurt soul—— or damned soul.

Hughie said: "You're welcome back!" and hurried out. "There'll be plenty of talk now", said the mother to Peter as he was eating happily with the knife and looking unimaginatively out the window with an analytical stare taking in the scene, thinking hard thoughts, Planning. Planning.

"I suppose so, Ma" he snapped.

"Tell them nothing. Let them fish for news. Too much the ould cobbler and Maggy Stanley will have to say. But you don't worry: there's no one can throw a thing at you."

As soon as Peter had his food taken he jumped up, stuck his stockinged feet in his boots and gave himself a shake as if freeing himself from everything in the shape of sentimentality. Like a lively weasel he moved across the floor. The mother was still talking softly but Peter wasn't listening. He went outside and standing on the green slope which looked south towards the Blaney Road he measured the fields within his vision and the people in them. He held the country in the palm of his hand.

His mind had been edged by exile. Abroad he had only been a labourer, but the knife of his thought that was too weak to cut through to success in a strange country would be sharp enough for this place.

There was wealth within his view, wealth that he would gather while all his neighbours were sleeping.

34

CHAPTER 3

That evening while Peter was walking alone, planning his future, the whole townland of Ballyrush was excitedly talking about the man who came back.

Off in the nearby bog John the Bard, a notorious character who spoke only in rhyme, had a visit from his neighbour Johnie Longcoat's mother who hadn't been on speaking terms with him for more than a year. She came to discuss the news. The Bard, who had been out breaking gravel for the road contractor, limped in on his crutches.

As we said, the Bard always spoke in rhyme. Once when he sued this very neighbour, he addressed the court:

My heart with indignation swells
As I state my case to Mr. Wells,
Alas, to tell about my bother,
With Johnie Longcoat and his mother.
I was in Scotland far away
When they drew home me cock of hay
And when I returned home I seen
Me stack of corn growing green.
He promised to thatch me mother's cot,
But no, he left it there to rot,
The rain came percolating through
And smashed a couple, sad to view....

These songs were naturally enough published in the local newspaper.

At the time of our story the Bard was engaged in the task of getting himself a wife and in defending his choice against the attack of other rhymers in the weekly newspaper. Because of this he hadn't the time or energy to keep up his spite against his neighbours, the Longcoats, who in fact lived under a common roof with only a low broken wall to keep their neighbourly hates apart.

So, he was not displeased to see Mrs. Longcoat (her real name

35

was Mrs. Mallon). The Bard opened up:

> The mother's pet is back again
> As far as I did hear
> And all the girls in Ballyrush
> Are filled with dread and fear.

"Bard, Bard," cried the admiring woman, "how do you think of it all? They may all take off their caps to you."

The Bard's pride expanded and his old mother sitting at the hob with a face on her as black as the back of the chimney, showed her pleasure with a low laugh.

"Rosie was telling me that Maggy Stanley saw him coming through Dooley's field and a big travelling bag with him."

> All with his travelling bag came Peter
> And that's the very best of metre.

"The man that had anything to do with poor Rosie will have a sin to answer for" said Mrs. Longcoat. "And will I ever forget till the day I die, or the day after," she mused on the winter's night— "and that was the stormy winter's night with the wind blowing and the rain splashing a total dread—— when this voice came to the door and said: 'Come down quick' says the man whoever he was for I didn't know at the time', 'come down quick to Mary Connor, she's very bad' says he, 'I'm running for the doctor', says he.

"I knew that she wasn't due for another month, but better to be sure than sorry so off I went in the middle of the night with the stable lamp in me hand through the bog. When I came to the house there was neither light nor sound. And wasn't that just the week before Jack Connor was sent to the asylum. He had that very night driven the wife and four young children out of the house at the point of a fork. Only the Grace of God and he'd have met me and put the fork in me. I found out who the blackguard was, Peter Devine."

> Oh, Mary, it's well I do remember
> That blustery night in late December
> When your brave life was risked to save
> A woman from a pathetic grave.
> Now I must go for to compose
> A song about my own sweet Rose
> To all good people she is known
> As **the** bright star of Culloville town.

"More of that to you," cried Mrs. Longcoat.

The Bard hobbled into a corner of the kitchen to continue his controversy with a rival Bard from up near Ardee. Apparently he had got second thoughts in joining a conversation unfriendly to Peter Devine. Although he made unfriendly and rude songs about fairly decent people he was inclined to avoid references to Peter. Too, the edge of his bardic satire was probably blunted by his own love affair with the girl from Culloville. Although he was a cripple with a bad reputation he was about to marry a young girl.

Some ten years earlier he had been to Scotland where he got injured and lost the power of his legs. Before that he was never known to have had any interest in bardic endeavours. In his prose life, as one might say, he was a crude lewd-spoken fellow, about forty years of age, powerfully built with a barrel chest and a large square head.

The people of the place thought him a great poet and even organised a football tournament to buy him a donkey and cart and set him up as a travelling haberdasher, selling delf, and pins and needles. Another football tournament was now being arranged to pay for his wedding. In the meantime everyone was disappointed that he had never really made up a good scarifying song about Peter Devine. Clearly even he was afraid of Peter.

On this same evening there was a crowd gathered in the shoemaker Conlon's house discussing the homecoming of Peter. Barney Conlon's establishment was the centre of parish gossip and Barney himself took great pleasure in orchestrating the story. He was married to a mild woman who spoke and walked in a timid manner. They had no children.

"I don't believe you when you say he'll stay," said Maggy Stanley who was present. "What is there for a man like that in this country?"

"He'll get a good wife, Maggy," said the shoemaker.

"But he hardly has any money."

"You'd never know."

"Now, where in God's name would he get it, Barney? unless he robbed somebody; out from that he can't have a brass farthing. I wonder who he might throw his eye on? Were you talking to him at all, Barney?"

"Oh, I had a few words with him" lied Barney in an off-hand manner, not wishing to admit that he wasn't on the inside of everyone's business.

Barney indeed had somebody in mind that Peter Devine might well throw his eye on but he wasn't going to tell Maggy Stanley or anyone else for that matter. Not now, anyway. She was Mary McKenna, daughter of the second biggest farmer in the parish. There she was, a girl of twenty-three or so, and sole heiress to a splendid farm of forty acres— if it was trusting to that. Through the window, when he raised his eyes, he could catch a glimpse of the tail of one of the fields with the three tall ash trees growing on the ridge of the hill.

CHAPTER 4

Peter Devine had returned without a pound in his pocket. But he had something better—— that ruthless edge on his resolution. He rose the following morning before five o'clock and took a walk through the fields. Fourteen acres of the best land, but there was no future in a farm of that size. Still it could be worked—— in a way.

The farm was in his mother's name. When dying, the father left it in her name feeling she would be the best judge of which boy should get it, when the time came.

Peter, walking in the dewy August fields —— among the whins that all the tilling in the world was not able to eradicate—— let his eyes and his mind sweep over the district. And just as the shoemaker had surmised, he thought of McKennas. He remembered the daughter, for he had his eye on her for many years and one of the things that made him sick as he was leaving the country was the knowledge that this girl was almost grown up. Wouldn't it be a terrible tragedy if after all his watching he lost her now?

He was also troubled about a sort of marriage he had contracted in Leeds. In a bout of drinking he had been lured into marrying the middle-aged woman with whom he lodged. As far as he could judge she already had a husband of some sort. If he could be sure of this, then the marriage was in fact not a marriage at all. He worried too if the shoemaker Conlon had got wind of this affair. The postmaster had, he knew, an uncle in Leeds. He would have to pump the shoemaker discreetly.

He returned to the yard around the house. His mother hearing him prowling around got up to make his breakfast. But he ate very little and snarled when she pressed a second egg on him. His mind was working too fast for eating.

"Aren't these other sons of mine the lazy good-for-nothings," the mother said aloud. "At least I reared one good son."

That same day the mother went about the neighbourhood

bragging about all the money Peter had brought home with him.

"He has handstacks of it," she told the shoemaker's wife.

"In that case, he'll get a good wife. Maybe Josie Duffy," Mrs. Conlon remarked with a show of innocence.

"Josie Duffy," sneered Mary Devine, "Is it a penniless girl like that? He could thatch a house with girls like that. Your husband Barney knows that." This latter remark to draw Mrs. Conlon.

"My husband tells me nothing, Mary. Indeed nobody knows half of the punishment I get from that man."

The shoemaker's loud voice came from the house: "Will you come in to hell outa that?"

Hurriedly she gathered up the nettles she had been plucking for the chickens and hastened inside the house.

"Who was that you had with you?" asked Barney.

"Mary Devine".

"And why didn't you ask her in in that case?" said Barney knowing Mary Devine would be listening.

"She was telling me of all the money Peter brought home," again spoken very loud for the benefit of her assumed audience.

Mary Devine was pleased at the response and moved up the road to spread the lie further about Peter's wealth.

A few days later Peter himself called on Barney Conlon. With a large smile on his face Peter entered the house. He overflowed the shoemaker with enthusiastic greetings and the shoemaker responded with equally dishonest effusions.

"Ah, holy smokes, ah, holy smokes! Peter Devine! Is it yourself that's in it? By the holy fly you took your time coming to see me. Take a sate. Mary throw on the kettle and make a drop of tay for Peter. By the holy farmer, Peter, you're the welcome man. What part of the world were you in at all?"

"Asking when he already knew the answer was what sent the devil to hell", says Peter.

"Now, Peter, how would I know where you were? Was it in America you were?"

"In Scotland, Barney; Glasgow," he lied.

"Aye, in dambut. Well, holy farmer! Peter Devine. And what's the bother?"

"Not a damn thing, Barney: I just called in to see you. Man, dear," he threw his eye on a pair of yellow boots that Barney was making, "who are they for?"

"For a dacent girl, Peter, and one that would keep the gutter from anunder any man. Who but Mary McKenna. And that's the girl that turned out to be the fine healthy lump. By the holy farmer, Peter, I tell you..."

He let his voice trail off. Seeing his wife was taking seriously his instructions to make tea for Peter he began to lilt his familiar:

Never heed it, don't mind it
Never heed it my dear.
Hit the big toe, hit the big toe,
Hit the big toe, my dear.

The wife at once caught the message.

"Peter, Mary McKenna is the girl for you."

Peter listened eagerly. The shoemaker struck the boot on which he was working with one final blow: "Farm of as good a land as there is in all Ireland. Forty acres...."

A young lad with a pair of old boots slung across his shoulders came in interrupting the conversation.

"What dunghill did you get these on, avic?" asked the shoemaker as he looked over the boots which had been made by his chief rival in the trade, Larry Maguire. "Never made a dacent boot in his life. Why don't you bring your repairs to the man that made them, gassan? Only your mother's a dacent woman I'd send you home with them. Come back in a month or so and I may have something done for you."

The boy went out. The shoemaker gave the old boots a contemptous stare and threw them in the corner.

"A healthy girl—— and a pious girl too, Peter. At the Altar every blessed Sunday morning. Be the holy living farmer if my own woman would take a notion to die I'd hang my own hat up there."

"But who are you talking about now," Peter says pretending not to understand.

"Mary McKenna, who else?"

At about this moment in the conversation the shoemaker found himself in the embarrassing position of giving good advice to someone he didn't like at all, or at least giving encouragement in the right direction. There was something in Peter's vicious mentality that compelled his enemies to help him forward. There were several other ulterior motives behind Barney Conlon's good advice. There was always the pleasing prospect that he might fail to win the girl.

Peter of course had his eye on McKenna's place even from the smokey distance of Leeds but at the best of times his thoughts about getting in there had not hardened into a practical plan until now. Seeing and sensing the possibility of succeeding, Peter felt somewhat astonished. In his wildest ambitions—— when hardy came to hardy—— he was just dreaming: he never thought of one of the parish aristocracy as a wife.

According to themselves—— and all social standards are self-set—the McKennas were well-bred people. They had a lofty contempt for the "scutch-grass farmers" of Ballyrush. But above even this consideration was the fact that they possessed their own turnip barrow, demonstrating their height above their neighbours. The turnip barrow was an implement which was used only one day in the year and for any farmer to have one entirely for himself instead of as a joint affair, was a moral staggerer. Even the Dooleys hadn't their own turnip barrow.

Peter Devine well knew that Tom McKenna's forty acres was rocky, whinny and rushy: being on the Louth-Monaghan-Cavan border it partook of many of the more unfortunate qualities of the two latter counties. Still, allowing for everything, the McKennas were in a class apart from the ordinary natives of Ballyrush.

"Ould Tom McKenna will be looking for a few pounds", said the shoemaker, "He's not too well off. And, not that I should talk about a customer, they are very bad pays."

Peter Devine said nothing. He was filtering out the lies and the malice in the shoemaker's conversation.

"Too many notions of high living," continued Barney Conlon; "trying to keep a horse to ride with the hounds like the Watsons. But whether or which, my advice to you Peter is that you could do worse than leave this matter in my hands. I'll be fitting these boots on Mary McKenna on Sunday at the forge after second Mass and I'll put a good word in for you."

"Good man, Barney," said Peter feeling that he had nothing to lose at this moment. The big news and the great satisfaction was that it seemed the shoemaker had heard nothing about his marrying affairs in Leeds. Of that he was fairly sure. Besides he realised that this was a common rumour spread about everyone who came from England or America. It resembled the ghost that always haunts the house that your rival hopes to buy. Peter was never put

42

off by such stories.

And so he went home to his mother's house and pulled himself together, shaking himself free from the soft flesh that the shoemaker's mind had grown on him. Barney Conlon's peculiar sympathy had a rotting effect on him. Once more he began to assert himself about the house. He began to order his brothers around. And they accepted his orders! He was not surprised at his power over them: it came natural to him.

"Four men about a place," he said to the mother one day in the presence of his brothers. "There's not work here for four men."

The road contractor, Mickey Fitzpatrick, arrived. His coming surprised the three brothers but not Peter. Peter had asked him to call over to take a look at one of the quarries that the brothers had been working at. The contractor and Peter went out together to look at the quarry pursued by the worried eyes of the brothers.

"Does he mean to sell that quarry?" one said to the other.

"To take any more stones out of the quarry will ruin the field at the back of the house. There'll be a hole there that'll be a danger to man and baste."

They saw Peter and the contractor bargaining at the face of the quarry but they were afraid to intervene.

"And why wouldn't he sell it?" said the mother; "who has a better right than him?"

None of the brothers had a reply to that.

Hughie went out and unhooked the scythe from the bush in front of the door and went down to the field of oats to start the harvest. The thought of anyone selling part of his farm shocked him. Selling the very stuff of the farm in the form of rocks and turf might bring in a few quick shillings but it would ruin those who came after them.

To make matters more tragic, since Peter had gone off to England the three brothers had restored some of the land already damaged by Peter, and drained off a couple of bog-holes from which Peter had sold hundreds of loads of mud turf. The three brothers, grief-stricken confided among themselves: they wanted, at least to advise Peter of the correct approach. But the mother told them to mind their own business when she heard of their ideas. "A body would think yous owned the place," she said.

"We have our share, Ma," said Hughie.

"The broad road and your health; that's your share" said she.

"A strange thanks that is after all we've done these past ten years," said Hughie. "That ould haveril went off and scandalised us all over the country with his dirty carry-on."

"Mind your own business, and don't let me hear yous saying a word against that good child. He's worth a cart-load of yous."

"Funny thanks," muttered Hughie.

"Go on out and do some work and don't be coming in here to abuse that good boy; a better or more goodnatured chap isn't in the country."

The brothers went off browbeaten, helpless in the face of their mother's affection for Peter and in the face of Peter's cruel power over everybody.

Mickey Fitzpatrick was a very big contractor and if he bought one of the quarries the Lord Himself wouldn't be able to calculate the number of tons of stones he would take out of it. Perhaps make a hole like the one in McKenna's field where the stones were taken to make the railway line. That would be a fine how-are-ye. But there was more to come.

Peter sold the rocks to the contractor, quarried and delivered to the roadside.

"And who is going to do the quarrying?" Hughie tentatively asked.

Peter dashed off without replying.

That evening he gathered a bundle of shovels, picks and crow-bars and took them to the forge. He ordered that they be put in good repair. Next day they were ready and he took them home. Next morning he had the tools laid out at the face of the quarry. As soon as the brothers had their breakfast Peter snapped in a voice like a rat-trap: "Quarry".

Hughie, emmeshed by love of the farm only made a mild protest and went docilely with the other brothers to do Peter's bidding.

Later on and with his thumbs in his braces Peter went out to see how his workmen were getting on. Three men, he decided, did not fit on the face of the quarry. "Tom," he said, "I have a job for you."

"What do you....?" Tom was about to question Peter but stopped short and put himself at Peter's command.

"Take the Blaney spade and cut a few perches of turf in the bottom of the field of oats."

Why were the brothers allowing themselves to be turned into

slaves? They did not really know. Their immediate fear was that the mother would transfer the farm to Peter and leave them in the right lurch.

Every day Peter made it his business to go through Dooley's fields by the old right-o'-way. He walked with a brazen air, and whistling a loud unmusical whistle in the hope that one of the straight-laced Dooleys would challenge him. But they shied off the encounter. Maggy Stanley watched him with delight. Her daughter Brigid watched too but with a longing for the disreputable Peter. Maggy Stanley kept up a continuous chatter about the possibilities of Peter's marriage to someone in the parish, totally disregarding her own daughter's hopes. Generations of slavery were in her blood.

CHAPTER 5

On Sunday the shoemaker with his size-stick in his pocket was busy in the forge taking people's measure for new boots.

By and by McKenna's back-to-back trap pulled up and the mother and daughter got down while the servant boy tied the pony to the ring-bolt in the forge wall.

"I have them here for you," said the shoemaker as the girl got down from the trap. "Will you fit them on now or wait till after Mass?"

Mary McKenna said she'd wait.

She tripped up to the church with her little short step and her jelly-like body and that pout of importance that she thought was her right to wear, her father being a forty acre farmer. Other women seeing her pass made rude remarks: "You'd think that one was keeping the teeth in us with the snarl on her."

Larry Maguire, a gawky youth of twenty-one was also watching Mary McKenna. He was in love with her and those that knew of this romantic attachment were amused, for love of this kind was very rare in Ballyrush. Larry Maguire's father also had this weakness some years back and almost threw himself in front of a train because of it. The shoemaker maintained that a weakness for this kind of love went with insanity and consumption. Certainly the poor and the wealthy never fell in love. Only occasionally the middle class.

The Bard believed in romantic love for every class. Wasn't he a poor man and wasn't he in love with the "star of Culloville?"

The old white-haired priest, Father Mullen, came up riding on his horse. He had bought that animal from the local horse-dealers and, in his own words, wasn't it a mane act that he the priest of the parish should have been done-in in a horse. The horse had side-bones.

The five Dooleys, three brothers and two sisters passed up to the church, all together and all prim, staring straight ahead.

46

Then Peter Devine appeared at the forge door. He made a gesture with an upraised finger, a horse-dealer's gesture, which meant nothing in particular except to give the idea of deep cunning—— a nod is as good as a wink.

"See you in the evening," he said to the shoemaker through his teeth.

After Mass Peter Devine delayed until most had passed down the road before sidling past the forge. He could see that Mary McKenna was there sitting on the horn of the anvil with the shoemaker fitting on the new boots. Already he was becoming possessive and he didn't relish the manner in which the shoemaker was holding the girl's leg. Peter never trusted a man who claimed to be doing another a good turn with a woman. And a man like the shoemaker, so fresh-faced and so outwardly pious was the worst. As Maggy Stanley had said: "I wouldn't trust a duck with that fellow."

But true to his word Barney Conlon passed along the message in an oblique manner to Mary McKenna. She didn't feel outraged at the suggestion and this looked good for Peter Devine. Peter visited the shoemaker next evening.

"I have everything fixed for you," said Barney. "I always said that it's easier catching an elephant than a hare. In this world, too, you should remember that the hardest thing to get is what you're entitled to."

"When are you going over to their house, Barney?"

"Oh, I wouldn't rush things, Peter. Nothing so dangerous as rushing...."

Their conversation was interrupted by the arrival of the Bard. His voice could be heard outside on the road. He came in. His presence was less than welcome but Barney put on a show of great good will.

"Me sound Bard, you're welcome."

All looked at the Bard who was somewhat excited. He told his tale in rhyme:

> If you'll pay attention in rhyme I will mention
> A story I'm thinking will interest thee,
> Although not a Nero some say I'm a hero
> In how I gave fight to a cad called McGee
> The welkin was ringing as off I went singing,
> For in Culloville I'm always well pleased for to be:

47

But in less than an hour, male, pollard and flour
Was whipped off me cart by consaity McGee.

"More of that to you," cried the enthusiastic poetry lover, Barney.

"Why don't you make a song about the Dooleys," asked Peter.

The Dooleys all both great and small
Have never done me harm,
My ass can stray all night and day
Around their dear old farm.

"Well, that be damned for a song," responded Peter.

The Bard wanted a new pair of shoes for his wedding. "Can you pay me?", asked Barney.

What 'er you say
The Bard can pay.

The Bard went off leaving Peter and the shoemaker once more alone.

"All is going well," said Barney, "All we want now is that you be able to put up a couple of hundred pounds. They have plenty of land but no ready money."

"I have nearly a hundred," said Peter.

"Then you didn't do so well across the water," said Barney delighted with the inside information and with the chance of holding something over Peter's head. "Anyhow, if you could knock up two hundred I think we'll manage it. There're plenty of others after the place but they haven't as much as would jingle on a tombstone."

"Aye, a poor eejut like Larry Maguire."

The shoemaker spat out a peg. "The very same, a penniless poor eejut. And not right in the head as well."

The upshot of the conversation this evening was that Peter decided to have his mother transfer the farm to him and then mortgage it up to the eyebrows.

When Peter drew around the subject to the mother about transferring the farm she readily agreed though she did say she would hold on to the house for the time being. Peter did not demur at this exception. He could get that later if he wanted it. Peter went to a lawyer and had the farm transferred, being careful to tell no one what he was doing - especially the shoemaker Conlon. He had told him too much already. In this kind of business -- involving over forty acres of land - a man was better working on his own.

Barney Conlon was too sweet to be wholesome. It was best that he be his own ambassador.

So it was that on Monday evening Peter rambled off in the direction of the McKennas. To deceive the shoemaker and other inquisitive neighbours who wouldn't let a man turn in his shirt without wanting to know the reason, he went down the lane towards the Dooleys and turned to the right past Maggy Stanley's. Maggy naturally enough saw him and rushed to speak.

"Musha, Peter, how are you? and it's you that is looking well".

"Making the best of weather, Maggy."

"They're kicking the ball in the meadow at the back of the hill; I suppose you're going there."

"That's right, Maggy."

"Aye, bedad! It's you that's doing well, not a bit interested in the girls like some of the other fellows here, Peter."

"It's well to be some people" said Maggy; "the poor women have to suffer all."

She was looking up the hill where the ragged form of the unfortunate Rosie could be seen as usual dragging a bush behind her.

"Look at that poor creature up there," she said, "that's to be pitied if ever a creature is to be pitied. Lord God! whoever had anything to do with that one has a sin to answer for. Went out of her mind altogether after you went away. Indeed, Peter, trying to blacken yourself, saying the bad drop was in all your people, even your father before you. Lord have mercy, I said, leave the dead alone."

Peter gave no response or reaction.

"Oh mean people," she continued, "even tried to say you married a black woman when you were away. Dirty low pack."

Peter listened carefully, quietly, and determined to remember. As he walked down the lane Maggy watched him from the top of the heap of dry mortar near the gable of the house.

At the crossroads he turned quickly to the right as if to go towards Crossmaglen; then when hidden by the bushes he wheeled around and crouching low went off in the opposite direction. He crossed the fence and going along the poplars and sallies was leaving the shoemaker's house on his right. Where was he bound for? thought Maggy. She could not see him but in what she did not see there was intelligence. She watched the openings in various parts of the hedges and if no figure darkened those gaps she knew at least where he was not going.

"Well," said Maggy reflectively to her daughter; "he must be going up to McKennas. Now what the damn devil would take him up that way? It's not for nothing he's on the march."

At that moment the middle-aged "Pancakes" with his hanging lantern jaws and general look of dejection came into Maggy's house to light his pipe at the fire. Paddy was a stonebreaker for the local contractor and was a relation to the already mentioned unfortunate Rosie.

"Did you see him," Maggy asked.

"I wouldn't look the side of the road he'd be on," said Paddy who, as Maggy happened to know was bitchy and mane enough to have taken a drink with him the evening before in the pub in Culloville.

Peter Devine, knowing nothing of this conversation and caring about its import only in so far as he was interested in the pattern of life as it is played, was at this very moment climbing up the backside of McKenna's hills. He climbed slowly and as he climbed his eyes were greedily examining the soil under his feet. It was such nice sweet land, so free and sandy and great for growing potatoes and oats. And great for milch cows too. Man alive, wasn't that a terrific field? He could hardly get **over** the size of it. There was in it the best part of four acres—— and only for the four or five rocks with clumps of blackthorn growing on them in the middle of the field there would be even more for the plough. Already in his mind, he had quarried those rocks and chased the silly fairies from their blackthorns. Wasn't old Tom the two ends of a fool to believe in such nonsense? At the top of the hill he entered the rings of an old fort. The land wasted by that fort wasn't less than half an acre. And the powerful trees growing there! Their value as lumber he calculated.

Down below him on the side of the hill opposite to where he climbed was McKenna's house. The long loft delighted him. Thirty yards long if it were an inch. That was a loft and a half! The dwelling house itself was a splendid slated two storeyed structure with the two chimneys, not as in vulgar houses with one at each gable, but here nicely placed one at the division between the kitchen and the west room, and the other at the side of the kitchen. Chimneys placed at the gable ends left the house half-frozen in wintertime. There was an upstairs window over the door in the centre and that was more quality.

Then there was the field behind the house! One of the best fields in the country; you wouldn't find better land than that around Ardee. Poor Tom McKenna was a fool, a bad manager, too fond of trying to live the life of a gentleman, riding to the hounds and acting the big-wig. Caught in the light of the setting sun the house looked golden. And golden it was in the eyes of Peter. Empty too, or nearly so; for ould Tom was about ready to die.

As Peter's eyes doted on the house and fields he saw Mary McKenna come out of the house with a milk can in her hand Peter's eyes followed her towards the far field. He thought he saw a man come from behind a hedge and follow her. His jealous anger stirred. With steps like knives cutting through the air he moved along the hedge towards where the man appeared.

As he came closer the man disappeared through a hole in the hedge and disappeared completely.

The girl was milking the cow. Peter stood behind the hedge in the hope of seeing the strange man. It could even be the shoemaker. Presently the girl got up from her hunkers, dipped her thumb in the froth of the milk and made the Sign of the Cross on the cow's flank. As she did so a fellow came from behind the ash tree in the corner. It was Larry Maguire.

"What the devil are you doing here?" asked the girl.

"You needn't think what you're thinking," he said. "I was coming this way in any case."

"Well, I wish you'd go some other way."

"I say...." he appealed to her as she walked off.

"What do you want?"

"Nothing, not a thing. I was only knocking around."

"You must be as mad as Johnie Longcoat."

"I'm not mad. I suppose I may go."

"And a good riddance too".

"It's a long road there's not a turn on," he said weakly. "You'll regret it yet. Mary! Mary!...."

Mary walked off as quickly as her short stride would let her and Peter saw Larry cross into the next field among the whins where he flung himself on the ground and began to eat the grass like a dog before a fall of rain.

How little the lad knew of women, thought Peter. How easy it was to succeed in a world composed of fellows like that. How any

51

fellow could have taken such a notion of Mary McKenna was a real puzzler to Peter. He himself was satisfied with her because she had the farm — and even with the farm she was no great bargain.

Anyhow, she looked to be a good worker.

Undoubtedly the young man was weak-minded.

He allowed her to go home without speaking to her. She was in too bad a humour now.

CHAPTER 6

As soon as Peter had the Deed to the farm in his hand he suggested that the brothers would find it more comfortable if they made a bed for themselves in the barn beside the cow-house.

It was coming on towards the chilly time of year and they didn't like the suggestion—— but it was either sleep in the stable or get out altogether. So the three men put up an old bed in the corner of the stable where there was a draught that would give galloping consumption to a polar bear.

Since the day he returned Peter had not done a tap of work but he gave the illusion of being a hard-wrought man. He was up every morning making a great commotion in the yard, rattling buckets, shouting, squealing, calling the dog, opening and closing doors. The three brothers had always been early risers but they could not compete with the energy of Peter. Even when they were not deceived into thinking that he was a busy man they felt ashamed of themselves sometimes when they heard Peter's shouting and squealing in the morning.

The neighbours began to respect Peter more and more. Everyone liked a man who got up early; it made their own lives seem less enslaved.

During the first few weeks of his return Peter had gone about in his best clothes. After that he became indifferent to his appearance and rushed around the yard in the morning with the front of his trousers unbuttoned and the bottoms stuck in at the back of his unlaced boots. He walked with his head out in front which helped to give the illusion of a man in a great hurry.

He began to develop a joking mind—— half joking and whole in earnest attitude when dealing with the neighbours and with his brothers. "Ha, ha, Hughie, you're up in time for your dinner".

As soon as the brothers got up he had jobs for them to do. He would have the two kicking horses harnessed and the two old carts heeled up so they would not be delayed while waiting for breakfast.

"Off to the quarry now and drive a couple of loads of stones before your breakfast, Hughie. You, Tom, carry them loose stones out to the haggard and make room for the rick of straw." Into the third brother's hand he would put an implement—— a graip or a shovel—— as soon as he emerged from his sleeping quarters. No one was delayed a minute.

Work was proceeding at a tremendous pace. The mother thought Peter a marvellous man. The lazy country looked on and admired more than ever that which they themselves lacked. Peter was getting on better than he had hoped, so well that he began to feel sorry that he had let the shoemaker in on his affairs. He was also beginning to think himself a fool for having worried about the McKenna girl. He was in fact too good for the girl, he thought, and when neighbours complimented him on how well he was progressing with the girl he laughed and said: "That's nothing: I could get the best of them with a wag of the little finger."

Peter intended meeting Mary McKenna on the following Sunday when the big football tournament in aid of the Bard's marriage fund would be held in McKenna's field. The McKennas always gave the meadow free but Peter had already decided that free or for payment the meadow would not be given when he took over control. Too dangerous for cattle with pins, needles and all sorts of refuse dropped during the game.

Sunday came.

From after last Mass on the Sunday the crowds could be seen coming across the hills from every direction as they converged on McKenna's meadow.

The Bard arrived with the goal-posts—— poplar poles—— in his ass and cart. He had his old mother with him and he was rhyming in all directions.

"I'll bet you couldn't make a rhyme about Greaghalattycapple?" a young boy challenged.

The Bard turned to his mother:

O mother, what an oul' townland, sure it rattles in me trapple,
I wish they'd ask an aisier one than Greaghalattycapple.

He made obscene remarks in rhyme to the girls. Everyone was in good humour.

Mary McKenna was going around the sideline very slowly in the company of Mrs. Kelly who had a son a Christian Brother and as a result was a cut above the ordinary person socially. During her slow march around the field Mary kept up a purse-proud growl and grumble, drawing loud attention to the fact that the field was theirs: "Only for us they'd have no place to kick, and the devil much thanks we get. Indeed some of the stuck-up people of the parish wouldn't have a bit to put in their mouths if it weren't for us...."

The Ballyrush football team was playing a team from the neighbouring parish of Donaghmoyne. The Ballyrush Boggums was a noted team. It was as much as a man's life was worth to make a disrespectful remark about these shin-breakers. A good football player—— that is to say a man who could maim the most members of the opposition team—— was the hero of the parish.

No politician on the climb could afford to ignore the football matches, no tradesman. It was a great day. The old men coming home from last Mass had by now adjourned their roadside arguments on politics, law suits and crime reports, and were hurrying home to a dinner of cold potatoes and re-heated cabbage before rushing off to the match.

Across the fields and hedges the football followers came, their heads before them, taking long strides. Their voices were loud and their behaviour serious-looking. The match was a serious affair.

"Would Pat Martin be playing for Donaghmoyne?"

"He got a bad kick of a horse the last fair of Blaney," I hear.

"He'll do his damndest to be here, just the same... I say, what the hell..."

They had come to a newly fenced gap.

"Who the hell put the buckwire in the gap? This is a right-o'-way to the well, I think."

"And a Mass pad too."

"Here, come over here. There's a hole in the hedge here."

Among this group was Jemmy Pepper and the shoemaker Conlon.

As they were seeking an illegal entrance they came across Peter Devine working his way through a hole in the hedge. Peter's innate meanness could not be supressed; he did not believe in paying to go in to such an event.

As it happened the man appointed by the Boggums' Football Committee to watch this particular fence was Frank Brady—— and they could not have got a more offensive man.

Barney Conlon joined Peter as the latter came through the gap and was settling his clothes. Peter had by now put on the face of a man who had given a large subscription at the entrance gate. He was a man whom only a very daring vigilante would approach.

Brady was coming towards Peter and Barney askew-wise across the green field from where the crowd was gathered around the edge of the pitch.

"Yez came in without paying", he shouted as he approached.

"Isn't that the right hure with his slobbering talk about us not paying."

Peter stopped to tie his boot and Barney was forced under demoralising conditions to face the bawling vigilante.

"It's a scandalous thing that a man of your manes begrudges the bare tuppence to get in," Brady said in the voice of a policeman.

"What the hell talk with you?" Barney replied from the tremulous cowardice of his conscience. He gathered some courage.

"Isn't it a damn foreigner like you that has the cheek to go for me, a man who was bred—— and all belonging to him—— in the parish you're standing in."

There was at least one mitigating circumstance—— Barney didn't think anyone in the crowd was within earshot of his public humiliation.

Peter, stooped, was enjoying the affair. This was the exact situation that appealed to him.

"Pay up," said Brady.

"I paid, I paid, I tell you."

"Who did you pay? How could you pay and me watching all the gaps on this side of the field?"

"I paid, and that's all. Why, you dirty little get, how dare you have the assurance to accost me like this. You that no one knows who you are or where you came from."

"Less of the ould gab. If you don't pay I'll have to put you out. Do you think it's for a cod I'm on these gaps since after second Mass. It would be hard to keep up a dacent team in the parish where there were many the likes of you."

"There's tuppence," said Barney at last. "And that's fippence I'm after paying the day."

Peter Devine was not asked for money.

"It's a long road there's no turn in," said Barney to Peter. "I'll get that hure's get if I have to wait forty years."

"Made a regular show of you," said Peter, "and with the world watching!"

This blow to Barney Conlon's pride and dignity turned him at once into an enemy of the local team so that when the match had started and the local captain was lying on the ground bawling "like a bull a-gelding" as a Donaghmoyne supporter expressed it, Barney felt no compassion.

Across the field, Frank Brady now acting as a linesman, was trying to keep half a dozen of the captain's brothers from invading the pitch and taking the Donaghmoyne man's life—— the one who attacked "our Paddy".

The line of spectators around the pitch was bulging inwards where the shoemaker Conlon was standing and the linesman tried to push the spectators back.

"He pushed you," said Peter Devine who was right behind Barney Conlon, "Begod I'd see him in hell before I'd let him off with it."

But Barney was no fool. He was not going to be pushed into a fight by a disturber like Peter Devine who thrived on maliciousness.

The rows at football matches were always an excuse for whoever had a spite to anyone, to give him a false blow from behind or, if he were a small man, from the front.

When the fights progressed beyond much reference to the football game into a series of family quarrels, the man who had no near relations but only the cold support of the team's loyalty was liable to be in for a bad time. Even a third cousin was more to be depended on than the closest friend. It was this value of family support that brought home to strangers in the parish—— or to illegitimates with no family connections—— the difference between the thickness of blood and water. Strong men, domineering men, were the men who had strong family support. A man could be a fool or a coward or a wild unusual person and be secure against the natural cruelty of the crowd to such a one, if he had many brothers and brothers-in-law and uncles.

Larry Maguire who was also at the match was forced into a fight by Peter Devine who was moving up and down the sidelines causing as much trouble as possible. Joe Meegan had his jaw stuck out and was challenging Larry Maguire to hit it. "Hit it a good wallop. Come on." Suddenly Larry hit it a softish clout. This was a signal for Joe Meegan's second cousin to leap into the ring and make a wild swing at Larry. Another cousin followed. Joe was taking his coat off and shouting "Who'll hould me coat? Will one of yez hould me coat till I hammer the lard out of this **get**."

Larry fought badly. It is not to be thought that an idealist makes a good fighter. An idealist with the poetic streak in him has too much of that questioning conscience that makes cowards of us all.

The curate of the parish who had arrived on the scene of this particular fight now interposed: "Are yous Catholics or savages? he shouted. He was only a small man but a lively one. "Disgraceful conduct for men calling themselves Catholics; yous have me ashamed."

The crowd sidled away. Joe Meegan tried to explain:

"Your holy reverence, Father, that I may never tell a lie and me at confession last Saturday week, but...."

"**But** nothing!" cried the priest. "You are an ignorant man and for two pins I'd let you have this umbrella across the shoulders."

That finished the fight and the priest departed for another part of the sidelines where someone was shouting "Take the hure's life." Meanwhile the game was proceeding.

Joe Meegan and his cousins realised that the young priest's conduct was "bloody well not good enough". That was taking sides among parishioners. But there was nothing they could do about it. Not now anyway. It wouldn't do to answer the priest back.

At the end of the match Peter Devine walked home with Mary McKenna. Their conversation ran roughly on these lines:

"Ah say, Mary" said Peter in the Portadown accent which he affected when he wished to give the impression of deep cunning— since many of the most cunning horse-dealers came from there; "thon's a powerful great hedge of bushes."

"Indeed they are," Mary drawled, "and they'd be a lot bigger only me father is always letting everyone cut them."

Peter toed the grass of the field: "Thon field needs a lot of dung, Mary. Ah say, what do you think of this Barney Conlon?"

"How?" came Mary's cow-like drawl.

"Ah'd say he's a bit of a blackguard."

"And who's not?" replied Mary bravely.

Peter dropped the subject.

Peter was a man who would chance anything with a girl but in the present situation he would be chancing too much were he to make an unacceptable move. The large fields were not to be gambled with.

"I hope them bastards are not following us," said he glancing back. He himself had often played the Peeping Tom and he did not trust others.

Nobody was coming: the fight in the meadow was still raging.

"Man dear," said Peter studying a young calf," that chap would make the right wee bull."

"This remark of Peter's gave Mary the chance to boast of the famous bull her father used to have:

"Watsons used to send their cows to be bulled," she said proudly. "And do you know? the crowds of people that got their cows bulled by me father and never paid him was a dread. Mane ould divils, go to every bull in the country and pay nobody. That was the costly bull on us. Half of the country owes us money on account of him but to see them now you'd think they were ladies and gentlemen of the land."

"A good bull" said Peter, "will bull twenty cows a day."

"A mongrel of a bull would," was her reply.

As Peter looked at her broad bottom in the evening light he thought of the great loamy meadow with the rise in the middle–McKenna's best field. When he noted her wobbling breasts beneath the loose blouse he dreamt of the field before the door with the deep hollow in the middle. Her black hair reminded him of all the lovely trees that grew on the property and the money he would make when he sold them. Every part of the girl was a symbol of her farm.

She was three or four inches taller than he was and almost twice as bulky. She laughed loudly at every remark he made but was disappointed at finding him so dull and tentative a lover. He was in love alright—— in love with the farm. She led him through a hay field and invited him to sit down beside her beside a cock of hay while she took off one of her new yellow boots that was pinching her. He sat down but made no amorous move.

Her soft gammy expression appeared to him like a full moon in rainy weather, and her spluttering lips were upturned like the lips of a new-foaled mare fondling her offspring.

Mary invited Peter to visit the house and he agreed to be over Monday or Tuesday.

As he walked home he stopped on a prominence to look over once more the property he expected to be his.

The northern side was heavy soil, marvellous for growing flax or wheat. Even the rocks and whins and useless stone walls became, as he thought of the property as his own, assets valuable and beautiful. A disused sandpit on the side of one hill with thistles and lush weeds of every description blooming there—— that wasn't something to be laughed at. It might perhaps be the most valuable part of the whole farm. The whins that grew in the sour soil were supposed to be good fodder for horses when they were pounded with wooden mallets. The briars that trailed in the drains and sometimes twenty or more yards out on the headland gave him all the thrill of a missionary come among the heathens.

Here in front of him was a field of Champion potatoes. Never, thought he, did he see such heads—— and where you have the heads you are bound to have the rest.

And a plot of turnips. Did anyone see such bad handling of what could be the best crop of turnips in the country? They had not been thinned out properly, nor had they been grubbed. Down the alleys was a mane of yellow weeds.

Peter sat on the headland between the potato and turnip plots and let the scent of the leaves do what they liked with him.

A mile in the distance was the corn mill. "Weren't the owners slack people," he said aloud to himself, the slack bloody people to let the mill go to the dogs; God, oh God!"

He stood up and surveyed the landscape. Ahead of him stretched the broad fields of Louth. The town of Dundalk was almost visible from here. Only for the haze he might be able to see the distillery chimney in Dundalk.

Then turning around towards the north he stared through the thick foliage of the whitethorn hedge and he surveyed the mean little fields of poverty. There was the shoemaker's house, and beyond that the hilly hungry townlands of Garlygobban and Kednaminsha where the horse-dealers lived.

What puzzled him most as he looked around was why some of the "smart fellows" hadn't pounced on such a good thing as Mary McKenna. Was it that they were afraid? Ah, thought he, a man needs to be away awhile before he can see what he left behind.

By Tuesday evening the match between Peter Devine and Mary McKenna was as good as made.

CHAPTER 7

"He'll make a spoon or spoil a horn," Maggy Stanley remarked to her daughter a day or two after the football match. "And I hope and trust you'll have no dealings with the ould haveril—— the mean low-down dog. The devil a thing he brought back with him to give any woman except what he has in his trousers."

"What do you think I am?" replied her daughter.

Peter Devine was coming up the lane.

"How are you, Peter?" says Maggy

"Keeping the best side out, keeping the best side out, Maggy. What's the news?"

"If you haven't something yourself how would you expect the likes of us to have news. By all accounts you are doing well for yourself, Peter."

"And how's that?"

"Oh, I do hear a thing or two, Peter. Poor Jack Dooley is taking it bad."

"Peter was about to express astonishment, this being the first time he had heard of the Dooley interest in the McKenna farm, but he did not let the woman know of his lack of information.

"And what has that fellow got for a woman?" he asked jokingly.

"Nothing as well proved as what you have got."

Full of excitement the daughter could not stay inside. She came out to the door, a pot-lid in her hand.

"I have no interest in the woman at all, Maggy," said Peter, "not a bloody bit."

"Oh, that will do you now, Peter, "you're not as green as you're cabbage-looking. Do you think the uncles will interfere? You know, that was their father's place...."

Maggy interrupted to call the hens, since a diversion such as this always gave her cutting tongue an improved slant.

"Juck, juck, juck! Are the hens laying at your mother's?"

"Didn't see an egg, I don't know the day or hour."

"Casting their feathers.... And young Larry Maguire I hear is after her as well. The poor chap hasn't got an ounce. What use would he be about a farmer's place."

A further diversion by Maggy Stanley: "Will you look at that shoemaker Conlon running around the garden to give himself a rest? A man I wouldn't trust with a duck.... Brigid will you run down and shut that gate and not let the Bard's ass ramble into our praties? And the postman Duffy is the man for the odd stories. Said he was reading in an English paper about a man who got ten years for marrying a second woman before the first one pegged. Would you believe a story like that?"

"Ould rubbish, Maggy, rubbish, that's all."

But all Maggy's efforts to shake Peter in his secrecy or his purpose were futile. He was strong. He wasn't trying to be happy and he wasn't trying to score over anyone unless such a score advanced his cause. Most of the people in the parish slandered their neighbours just for the fun of it. The flamboyant phrase or the subtle dig interested him not at all.

CHAPTER 8

Mary McKenna wanted to be married quickly, and it had been arranged that herself and Peter would tie the knot as soon as he had his corn threshed and the potatoes dug.

The time now was the month of October.

Peter had his three brothers hard at work digging the potatoes and now he was waiting for the mill-man to say when he could come. Up to this time no steam thresher had ever been up the Garleygobban lane but this year Peter was determined to have the steamer and not the old horse-mill.

He called on the millman who was threshing for a man out on the Blaney road. This mill-man was a sour fellow who, because he had the only mill in the country, took delight in insulting all farmers who had less than a day's threshing when they came looking for the mill.

"Me oats is heating," a poor man was saying while Peter looked on waiting to ask him.

The mill-man threw a shovelful of red clinkers into a pool of water at the man's feet sending a puff of hot steam into his face.

"What am I to do?" pleaded the fellow.

"What do I care what you do?" Get the flail."

Even though Peter had only half a day's work the mill-man was quite friendly to him, even deferential. He could give Peter a promise for the following Saturday afternoon, if that was any use.

"But how am I going to get up the lane?"

"I'm getting a run through McKenna's fields."

"It's well to be you but hard to be like you." said the cranky mill-man with some hint of a smile.

Peter returned home through his potato fields where the withered stalks were silvery white and the brown clay like dust in the dry wind. His brothers who were digging put on a spurt as he approached but he passed them without speaking. He was wondering at that moment how best he could keep the two farms going.

If he could rent the place to the brothers for so much a year he might be better off than running two places.

"You must be tired," said the mother when he got back.

"The steamer is coming on Saturday after dinner," he said.

"Isn't that great?" said the mother. "Won't that madden the Dooleys? Here, take this sup of tay before the others arrive."

Excitement ran high in Garleygobban when the steam thresher chugged through the fields on Friday night—— the mill-man having finished the previous job sooner than expected. A crowd of young people followed the machinery. The mill-owner with his blackened face made it his business when he came out on the narrow lane at the end of McKenna's field to knock down as many gate-posts of the small farmers and cottiers as possible.

The spirit of a pioneer was abroad. Since the beginning of time nothing more heroic than a horse thresher had replaced the flail. The age of steam had arrived in Ballyrush. Peter walked in advance of the engine swinging a lantern and telling the driver where to go.

"Oh, me clamp of turf," cried a poor man, as the wheel of the engine knocked the side out of a turf pile.

The thresher was set up in Devine's small haggard that night. Peter's three brothers were every bit as proud as Peter himself and they were inclined to take some credit for it. When Peter wasn't listening they told neighbours how they had made the haggard so sound that no machinery however heavy would sink in it. They had put hundreds of loads of stones in the spot where the dung-hill used to be.

The wind was rising. The moon was being blown about like a kite in the clouds. A cheer went up and Peter himself joined in because he knew that the carnival spirit was an incentive to work.

At seven o'clock the next morning the whistle of the engine calling the workers to the threshing could be heard over the townland. Looking out their front doors Maggy Stanley, Barney Conlon, the Bard's mother, and a dozen others who were early risers could see the three brothers on top of the rick stripping off the old bottom hay which covered it as a protection against rain. The escaping steam and smoke rising from the engine into the crisp frosty air in that peaceful country was something to remember for a long time.

The workmen soon began to arrive with their pitchforks on their shoulders. There was nothing like having plenty of help and

Peter had sent the youngest of the brothers around the country earning swop help at all the local threshings. Many came who hadn't been earned and among these was Larry Maguire. Peter saw him coming up the lane from the crossroads, a little lonely-looking without a fork. He was gazing dreamily at the bright straws that were trellised on the trailing briars of the narrow lane where the loads of corn had been jammed. Peter decided, at that distance, that he would put him carrying the bags of oats and would see to it that they were well packed.

Larry came of course in the hope of meeting Mary McKenna. In this at least he was not to be disappointed for Mary was on her way up the lane ahead of him. She would be directing the cooking.

Brigid Stanley also came for the same purpose but when Peter saw her he at once put her pitching sheaves since, as he said, she would not be needed at the cooking.

The machinery hummed. The dust and chaff began to fly. Peter was anxious to have the job finished at about half-eleven so there would be no need to give the men a full dinner. "Just a sup of tay will do," he told his mother.

Peter was a great believer in giving workmen large quantities of weak tea when their spirits began to flag. He practised this policy when dealing with his brothers and with the road contractor when he visited them on business. One would think he was giving out glasses of whiskey, for as they sat around gulping the blue-head tea he kept up an elaborate show of high spirits.

The mill-man was paid by the number of sacks threshed and Peter saw to it that the bags were well packed. Besides, he had hired the largest sacks he could find. In addition to saving on the threshing bill it pleased Peter to see that he broke the back of Larry Maguire carrying the overfilled bags up the loft steps.

Peter kept scooting in and out among the sheaves, the machinery and the chaff, popping up out of nowhere when some man was thinking of taking a smoke.

"Ha!" Peter would squeal, "Want to burn the haggard?" The fellow would slip the pipe quietly into his trousers pocket.

The threshing was finished at half-past eleven in the morning.

"Now, in for tay with you, boys," he kept saying to every man he met as if he were doing the big thing. Some growled at there being no drink, but there was no mutiny.

The Bard's mother came with a tick for chaff and she was

filling it as the men went in for tea. Presumably this was to be the Bard's marriage bed.

McKenna's threshing was on the Monday. This was a bigger job, one which lasted from early morning till late night. Peter took charge as if he already owned the place. To finish the job they had to work in the dark. During this time a number of young women arrived to see and be seen, as the saying went. Young men were pursuing them and there was much screeching in the still night air. There was one young girl present who was not taking part in the carouse. Barney Dooley was discussing her with Peter Devine. Bit by bit he was putting it up to Peter that he should make a tear at her. Peter finally gave in and off he went towards the stables where this young girl had gone. At the same time Mary McKenna was seen disappearing behind the ricks with an unknown person who could be Tom Duffy, the postman.

Peter continued his vain pursuit of the girl. He coaxed and he pleaded but she giggled and led him round the carts and stables till in the end he didn't know whether to follow his idea to its logical end or cut his losses. He was making a fool of himself—— or rather the little flirt of a girl was making a fool of him.

"Come here," he would appeal.

She would run off a short distance and stop.

"I tell you stop!" he would say as though he were speaking to a servant girl.

The most Peter was hoping for now was that he should find some excuse to save himself from this embarrassing situation.

He finally mustered his courage and turned right about hoping that he could escape without being seen.

As he returned to the thresher who did he see emerging from between the rick of straw but Mary McKenna and Tom Duffy. He was at the moment trying to put on an edge of manliness after being so degraded by the little flirt—— and now this. Before Peter had time to say a word Duffy rushed up to him:

"Your rick of straw was going to the hollow," he said, "only I saw it in time it would have gone completely."

He turned his eyes up to where the men on the high rick were silhouetted against the moon and shouted: "Keep well to this side; she's going to the hollow."

Peter was not deceived but on the other hand he was glad that at least no one had seen him make a fool of himself. The incident wouldn't have done his marriage chances any good.

CHAPTER 9

In spite of everything and everyone—— the Dooleys, Barney Conlon, the Maguires—— Peter's marriage arrangements prospered. Every evening he visited the old man and talked to him about horses. Like the average Gael, he knew little about blood horses and cared less—— except in so far as he might make a few pounds out of them. Old McKenna was no expert either so both blathered away. The old man was easy to impose upon. Usually Peter Devine boasted by means of making the poor mouth but in this instance he found bare-faced boasting much more successful. He talked in hundreds, even thousands and the old man soaked it up with relish.

So gentle did he look with his milky complexion and snowwhite locks that Peter calculated he hadn't long to live. One bad winter would finish him off. He was well-preserved but of the type that can easily go off like a shot.

Barney Conlon avoided Peter those days despite his excessive curiosity. He sought his information mainly through Maggy Stanley and others with a reputation for gossip. He was afraid of Peter.

Then one morning Tom Duffy, the postman, who had a cousin in Leeds, got word that Peter actually had been married. He told Maggy Stanley in confidence who in turn told Barney Conlon pledging him to the darkest secrecy. And though the word got around no one was prepared to say so publicly, so fearful were they of this ruthless character.

Peter Devine was married in the middle of November. It was a hard sunny day and there were lots of cars. The wedding procession went the usual route through Dundalk and Cross and home again—— everyone by then well drunk, except Peter who merely pretended drunkenness so he could better pump everyone in the party. He slobbered over everyone and kept putting his arm around all sorts of women whom he met on the tour. Everyone thought him a real gay fellow.

As soon as the married couple arrived home that evening they saw at a glance that trouble was in the air. The two uncles, accompanied by another man, had taken possession of the house. They already had abused the old man for handing over the place to a stranger. The poor old geezer was now upstairs in bed and very ill.

Peter left his bride and other members of his entourage back some distance in the yard while he himself went up to the door and peeped in. The three men in possession had armed themselves with three large brass candlesticks and were strutting belligerently about the kitchen floor. Peter was afraid of no man provided that man were drunk and he could be taken by surprise. But none of these men was drunk.

While Peter was surveying the expected battlefield his three brothers who had kept well behind in the wedding procession—— not wishing to associate with the drunken members—— came forward. Peter explained the situation.

The brothers were not cowards but their policy was to avoid fights if possible. Peter changed that policy. He ordered them to clear the house. Each of them took a piece of plough iron from a nearby wall and went in the door which oddly enough was not barred. It was a fierce fight. One of the brothers got a wallop of a candlestick and this so infuriated the other brothers that within a few minutes they had the uncles beaten and ready to surrender. At this point Peter entered carrying in his hand a sweet eight-ounce stonebreaker's hammer with an ash-plant handle that had a spring like a whalebone. Calmly while his brothers were still wrestling with the uncles he went to each of them in turn and gave them a neat tap on the skull with this hammer. He judged his taps well, not so hard as to break the skull and not too soft that the uncles might be able to fight again in any decent length of time. Neighbours, who were not relations, stood outside in awe. Here was something as awful as a family fight at a wake. This was something to be remembered forever.

During the following weeks there was much talk about the fight and the curious fact was that it was Peter and not his brothers that got the credit for beating the bullies. There was no mention of the hammer, though there was of the candlesticks.

"Only he had some poor body's blessing—— and if ever a lad

earned a poor body's blessing it was that good son of mine," was how Peter's mother saw it.

The Bard was called upon to make a song about the battle but he made the excuse that he was presently occupied in the afore-mentioned controversy with his rival Bard.

ii

Peter—— though he signed nothing—— agreed to surrender his claims to his mother's house on condition that he got the double plough, the saddle harrow, the blue cow and several other items of rarity and value in that society. He assured his mother that she was now independent of her family, having two homes, and that if she chose she could come and live with him. The mother assumed that this offer derived from a deep generosity in her son's nature. She would stay where she was, she said. What did an old woman matter? she remarked to a curious neighbour. "That was the good son!"

Peter stripped the place bare, didn't even leave the old wooden grubber with the brothers. The mother stayed where she was and, with her other sons, lapsed into deeper poverty—— and from the point of view of this story, into total obscurity.

The farm which Peter married into was as good a farm as was in the country. Ten four-acre fields—— with a drink in every one of them. The wife that went with the property was no fallen goods either. She was, it is true, a bit of a trollop, a big slop of a girl with light bones that would be liable to cause her to fall into what the local people would describe as "a fierce hape."

For the present, she was not unattractive. In the presence of her husband she felt as a rabbit must feel in close proximity to a weasel. The result was that she tended to do in public what she feared to do in private—— and so, among other things, she boasted a lot to the neighbours. Yet she had a soft drawling voice and a slow way in everything while at home.

Peter's first job was to re-survey his newly acquired farm—— this time accompanied by his father-in-law. The farm was protected on all sides by high, untrimmed hedges with briars extending well out into the fields. There were several overgrown forts which every-one regarded as sacred to the fairies and were never to be intruded on or ploughed.

Peering in among the stems of the blackthorn and the mountain ash Peter observed the huge boulders of whinstone, moss-covered, that stood up like tombstones. John McKenna looked too but in a different light. Here was the home of the leprechauns and the fairies. If a fairy were to hop out in front of him he would be disappointed rather than excited since his faith would be diminished by the gross actuality of their mere mortal existence.

"There's half an acre of waste on this field—— if it's trusting to that," said Peter.

"There's plenty of land for everyone and for everything," commented old McKenna.

Peter wasn't listening. He was studying the quality of the stones. "If they could be quarried...."

John McKenna was troubled. If he could only tell his son-in-law of the futility of land-greed! But somehow Peter Devine had a poisoning effect on his mind so that whatever he thought of saying seemed silly even before he uttered a word. No use talking to him about the weird-rooted memories that were in those fields. No use telling him that the great Clan McMahon live here, or that the last head of the family with his fifteen sons rode on sixteen snow-white horses into the town of Louth on one occasion. Were he to mention that story Peter would surely inquire if they were going to sell the horses at the fair.

"What kind of people put up these hedges?" he remarked with scorn: "you'd think they were trying to write their names with the fences."

The survey convinced Peter that not less than one-third of the farm was waste. He intended to change all this.

iii

For two months after his marriage Peter let things run quietly without change until he developed a grip on affairs.

The three men who had been working regularly for years for the McKennas were, in the opinion of all decent men, "As lazy a set of loorpauns as ever slept on a headland."

They were too lazy to bless themselves. They wouldn't rise in the morning till the sun would burn another hole in their arses. These were a few of the remarks made by the small farmers of the locality. A lazy man was the lowest creature a farmer could imagine. To be up early working in the hay or the clay— — even if you were doing more harm than good— — was considered the ideal.

Peter was not overly worried about this laziness, nor did it concern him that one of them was small and miserable looking. His theory was this, that no matter how lazy a man might be, provided he was kept going, he'd get the work done. He had no use either for the man who made a bit of a rush and then took a rest.

He never let his men in on him: they never knew the night before what particular job was to be theirs the following morning. He planned out everything by the minute.

One morning going out to the haggard Peter found the three men staring up with dreamy eyes at the well-built pikes of hay. He scratched the bony back of his head and made a low squeal.

"What do you think of them? Aren't they worth looking at?" said one of the men, a tall fellow called Joe Toal, who had recently got married.

Peter looked up at the pikes with the ruthlessness of a man who was not in love with anything.

"Were they built for looking at?" he asked.

"Good looks never did anything any damage," said Joe.

Peter, however, took a liking to Joe. He looked like a spirited fellow who could be excited into doing two men's work. He wasn't enthusiastic about the two other fellows who were much older and who had been farm labourers all their lives— — experts in the art of killing time. They had said nothing about the pikes of hay but kept walking around them as if they were planning something important.

"Build that wall, there," Peter said to one of the two.

The man trotted off to examine the slightly broken wall of the haggard.

"And you, clear away the briars and weeds in the back yard," he said to the other.

"But them's the flower beds," replied the fellow.

"Clear the weeds away,"

"And what are you going to put there?" the man asked.

But Peter was gone off towards the horses' stable. The fellow continued to call after Peter inquiring why he was supposed to clear the back yard where the flower beds were.

Peter turned. "Now, what do you want to know for?" he asked.

Explaining the reason for things, according to Peter not only wasted time but tended to confuse the minds of the workers. The old labourer was unhappy: there was no satisfaction in doing a thing when you didn't know the reason for doing it.

At the end of the day the two men were, in their own words, "not able to give their sowls to God or man." And the strange thing was that they hadn't noticed themselves doing more work than usual; they had merely been kept moving. No sooner was one job finished than Peter had another one ready. They hadn't to wait around after dinner till the master had made up his mind what was next on the agenda. One second after they had their food gobbled- - - - -and even in the matter of eating Peter encouraged no superfluous masticating-- Peter said to one of the men: "Take this shovel" -- he had the implement in his hand with the point newly sharpened-- "and clean out that gully at the bottom of the dunghill while we are putting the horse in the cart. You carry them stones that's in the yard and leave them beside the wall," he said to the other.

The two men hurried off to their appointed tasks, the old fellow who was ordered to move the stones was wearing a miserable face for he wondered how on earth he was going to remove the stones, each of which weighed no less than a hundredweight. Peter, standing in the doorway, looked after him and smiled a thin smile. He saw the labourer struggle with a bolder and was satisfied that he was fit to carry any of them if he put his heart in the work.

Peter and Joe took the horse and cart and Joe was ordered to drive to the bottom of the stubble field. Peter went ahead on foot, opening gates and glancing about him at this and that.

"What are we going to the stubble field for?" Joe asked innocently.

Peter, continuing his training of his labourers not to ask questions, made an irrelevant remark and walked on. They collected some bushes that had been thrown into the sedge on the edge of the lake which then was white with the silver of autumn, so quietly mysterious.

By Christmas Peter found one of his men undrivable. He was stubborn as a mule: neither flattery nor tea at ten o'clock in the morning and after dinner could induce him to lose his fear of doing too much. Peter sacked him and employed Jemmy Pepper the stone-breaker, a man with the reputation of making his master's thoughts his own. It was Jemmy one wet day in December, feeding the pigs, that suggested to Peter that he should keep a boar. Peter listened without any apparent interest—— never wishing to concede to anyone that he accepted or even recognized as having heard a good idea. Later on Peter raised a boar.

During the first year of his marriage no working day passed that the sound of crow-bar and pick on stone was not heard in Devine's fields. In the spring one man was ploughing while the other two men were quarrying or trimming the whins and briars. Jemmy Pepper was so excited by his master's ambition that he was known to have taken a crow-bar on a Sunday afternoon to one of the rocks. He would deny this breach of the Sabbath very strongly, for he was full of traditional devotion. Jemmy believed that when he was working for Peter Devine he was working for God.

"A dacent man, Jack, and I never found him anything else."

"A bloody slave-driver."

"Slave-driver be damned. I never knew him to ask a man to do what he wasn't willing to do himself, Jack. I never yet bet him in getting up in the morning."

Jemmy was explaining to Peter's second workman the advantages of being Peter's employee.

"You are never hard-set until you have to keep to the clock," he said as he grunted and pounded the rock with a heavy bar.

iv

It was nine o'clock one evening in May. From half-past five that morning they had been up, driving and spreading dung in the drills for the turnips. When the last drill had been closed at half-past six in the evening Jemmy suggested it was too soon to knock off. "Anyway, a change of work is as good as a rest," he said. "Let's go to the quarry."

Peter himself had taken the pony and was now finishing the sowing of the turnips—— a simple and interesting job.

"The cool of the evening is the right time to sow turnips," said Jemmy as he moved off with the crow-bar.

Over in the hollow they could see old Barney Dooley driving the cows in to be milked. Through the gate of the field in which they were now working Peter's wife came with a tin navvy-can in one hand and a packet of bread in the other. She was bringing

73

them tea. This was on her husband's orders.

The thought of the tea arriving made Jemmy— and even Jack— ashamed of themselves for not having worked harder. Their spirits rose and love of a most heroic kind filled their souls —— for their master. Scalding hot tea it was and very blue in colour as if the milk put in it was skim milk. The bread was home made and had an unbaked stripe up the centre. But the men were happy and grateful and would show their gratitude by working harder and longer that evening than ever they had worked before.

Mary McKenna was largely pregnant but neither of these men took notice of—— or pleasure in—— her condition. They had never thought of anything like that. The local neighbours having knocked-off early were over at Ballyrush crossroads or down at Tommy Fitzsimon's public house. Their shouting and laughter echoed in the calm valleys. The snipe fluttered over the swamps. The fields were whispering of life.

Up and down the drills went Peter driving his fast-moving pony. Darkness had fallen when he unyoked the animal and came slowly down along the hedge.

The quarry-men watched him.

"Yez did enough for one day," he shouted.

Jemmy pretended not to hear so that he could demonstrate his intense interest in his work.

"That's a very easy rock to split," he said

Crack, crack, crack, the bars went.

"A man couldn't be at a nicer job," he sighed.

"Come on in outa that," Peter called again as he went through the gate into the yard. The men waited a decent time before going. Then with their tools on their shoulders they trudged home, happy and proud of their day's work.

Sitting at midnight drinking weak tea Peter was straining for the next day's dawn. He was planning the next day's work, every half, indeed every quarter of an hour. There was a stone wall half-down between the Black meadow and Dooley's corner: the sooner that was repaired the better. The boar was ready for service. He would have to get the shoemaker to write out a notice advertising the fact to stick up outside the chapel gate on the coming Sunday. It was a pity he hadn't decided on keeping a bull or a stallion. But better wait and see how the boar worked out.

The pair of workmen struggling up the stone steps to their

74

ruckety bed in the dusty corner of the loft did not realise that they had filled a day to the utmost of two men's capacity. Joe was asleep in the corner after having helped with the milking and other household jobs.

"It's very chilly," remarked Jemmy as he stood in his bare skin looking down at his companion in bed. "Amn't I better throw an extra pair of trousers at the bottom of the bed? Did yez see me Sunday trousers?"

They're over there on the bag of oats."

"Jack, Jack, get up!"

Jack shook his bottom petulantly with the exasperation of a sleepy child.

"Sure, it's not that late," he grunted: "the hens are not let out yet."

"Get up or we'll be the talk of the country."

Peter was up. In the yard he was creating the commotion of a mid-day farmyard, rattling buckets, scraping out stables, shouting at the dog. Jemmy stooped down and looked out one of the slits that served as windows.

"Maybe the cow is after calving," Jemmy said, "and wouldn't it be a nice how-do-you-do if something went wrong and us lying in bed. Get up Jack, ye lazy hure, ye."

"You'd drive a man mad," said Jack, and raising in bed he reached for his shirt which hung on the winnowing machine at the foot of the bed.

Peter left the yard with the dog and climbed the hill in front of the house to have a look at the cattle on the back hill. The cow, which he had seen earlier, was in no danger of calving yet. Over on a hill opposite, one of Pat Lennon's men was catching the horses..

Pat is a greedy man, thought Peter. A greedy man indeed. No wonder people say the devil attacked him as he came home from the fair and left him a-show-to-the-world with a broken nose and several teeth knocked out. He was Peter's enemy and rival. Peter was aware of the jealousy, envy and hate but his instinct told him that these evil thoughts do more harm to the person who holds them than to those against whom they are directed. The right way to break a neighbour's heart was to succeed oneself. The only player at cards who plays well is the man who keeps his eye on his own cards. It was an old principle of card playing.

Peter toed his cattle till they stood up. They seemed in good health. He went towards the corner of the field where Dooley's garden stuck its triangular patch of weeds into his good field. Between the field where he stood and Dooley's yard was a dirty stream. It was unlucky to have a stream flow before the door, very lucky if it were flowing behind. Such nonsense, he thought. The Dooleys were poor, not because of the stream, but because they lay in bed too long in the morning.

As soon as the two men had breakfast taken that morning the master said: "Take them pair of mallets and break the lumps in the potatoes."

The pair of mallets stood beside the dresser. This was the first time either of the men had seen the tools and did not know that they were to be sent to this work.

They started breaking the hard clods. The sun shone brightly; the birds were singing in the clear sky. From the Railway Works at Dundalk the buzzer blew at five minutes to six.

"I wish I had a job at the Railway Works," said Jack.

"Ye have a better job where ye are," Jemmy said in a very wordly-wise tone. "You have six shillings a week here and all found, and the life is not dragged outa ye."

The day wore on.

Nothing particular happened on that day or the next day. It was just life going on and a little man hurrying to keep up with it.

CHAPTER 10

Peter was doing a fine trade with his boar. The shoemaker had written out the notice: "Boar for Service" and posted it up on the wall beside the chapel gate.

That was weeks ago.

Every Sunday, Peter and his wife drove on their side-car to Mass in Ballyrush. Peter was what was known as a good man for a lift. So long as there was space on the car he never passed by any Mass-goer. As far as possible he managed to give lifts only to mothers who had rising families fit, or nearly fit, to work on a farm. He never passed Mary Toal if she could at all be crushed on to a seat. She had a large family.

Mary said that a decenter wee man than Peter Devine wasn't standing within the walls of the parish. She said so to Maggy Stanley whom Peter had never carried to Mass. Maggy did not agree.

"A dirty little dog, he is," said Maggy spitting out," "a ferret-faced rascal that will be in the low pits of hell before he's half dead. Is it just because he gives you a lift in that ould car of his that I wouldn't trust for a minute, that you think so much of him? That's a poor way, and a low way, and it's no way...."

Maggy stopped her tirade to address herself to the two illegitimate children of Rosie Malone's that were coming along the road with a can of milk.

"Ah-ha! that's the right boy and girl," said Maggy turning to the two children. "Aren't they getting very big? Bringing home their can of buttermilk".

The children had stopped in a somewhat frightened pose a few yards apart from the women.

"And where did yous get the milk, little girl? she asked.

"In Dooleys" the girl replied.

"And I bet you have a swimmer in it," Maggy said going over and lifting the lid off the can. "Ah-ha! That's what it has, a lovely rowl of butter." She replaced the lid.

"Who do you think they take after?" Maggy asked Mrs. Toal.

"The girl is a daughter of Gernon the stationmaster that used to be in Ballyrush, as sure as you're a living woman. She has his eyes. It would be hard to say who owns the gassan. Oh, the man that had anything to do with that unfortunate Rosie Malone has a sin to answer for."

"Isn't she lucky to have such a pair of children? It's a pity the first one, Peter Devine's, died of the measles. Aye, is she lucky!"

Time was passing slowly, changelessly in the little fields. One day followed another and the tomb opened as naturally as the womb.

No day passed that Peter Devine hadn't two or three sows for the boar's service. The service was only a shilling but even so it kept him handling money. The man who has the handling of money can become rich easily enough by merely holding on to what comes to him —— holding every penny he can.

Peter was willing to give credit to poor men with children fit to work just as he gave lifts on his car to such people. Hardly a day went by that Pat Dooley did not come looking for the loan of something. Sometimes it was the cart or a yard-brush, or sometimes it was for a few shillings. Peter seldom refused. So it was that in the harvest rush Peter had more help than the biggest farmer in the parish. While others were about to reap their oats, Peter had it already headed in stooks safe from the weather.

"The cart," said Peter to his workmen after dinner on a very wet day. Jemmy took the cart and all of them went to the quarry. A few more short signs and the men began loading the cart. When it was full Peter walked rapidly before the horse and led the way to the cart-pass. Here the loads were dumped, hundreds of loads as the days passed—— for this happened to be the wettest week in memory, weather unfit for much else to do around a farmer's place.

Peter was making a new road, a short-cut to the main road. When his wife was asked by some old friend at Mass what sort of a lane he was making she answered: "It's not a lane, it's an avenue!"

One would think Peter was trying to be contrary when he marked out the lines of the new avenue. It ran straight through the softest part of a swampy bottom where beneath the seemingly innocent green grass were old bog-holes where a horse might sink and never be seen again. Had he chosen to run the road a little to the left he would have firmer ground. Peter, however, had his own ideas.

Returning from having emptied the load of stones Peter saw to it that the workman, cart and horse paid tribute to the passing day. A load of dung was to be carried back. To be able to jog back in an unloaded cart, singing while he stands up in the swaying vehicle, was one of the things that made going with the load worthwhile. It left room for hope. But instead of hope Peter supplied watery tea.

The work went on. The corn was sown and the potatoes planted.

In the evenings of April the three men spent their time from seven in the morning till nine at night uprooting blackthorns, boortrees and briars and quarrying the rocks under them.

Everyone said that Peter would rue the day he uprooted those fairy rocks and lone bushes. They did not dare say so to his face, for Peter was becoming a man so reserved, so frighteningly important that simple folk recoiled from him. Maggy Stanley referred to his desecration of the forts one day in Barney Conlon's. Jemmy Pepper was present.

"I'd rather you be doing it than me, Jemmy."

Jemmy spat in the fire in the manner of his employer and replied that all that talk of fairies was a cod. Barney Conlon told several stories of men who were as independent in their time as Peter. "There was a man," he began reminiscently: "there was Henry McArdle, yous all remember and he was going on like that too. And we all know what happened to him. The way that's in it, a thing that's not hurting you, leave it alone. And the cobbler went on to talk of other tragedies resulting from the ill-will of the fairies.

In due course Peter heard all this retold by Jemmy, his faithful slave. But he was not angry. Neither was he amused. He was contemplating other things, the things that lie below the romantic surfaces, the hard cores of men and women that a man only comes into contact with when he—— having been strong and a tyrant—— is down.

On this calm evening he wandered through his fields looking at the quietly grazing cattle, watching up the hills where the drills of young potatoes with their young buds were breaking through. He went down on his knees and shutting one eye gazed along the drill. He could see the row of buds coming up. Here was a gap in the row. He buried his fingers in the dry soil and searched. Searching for a hidden bud and finding it ready to break the surface gives a man the thrill of the miracle of birth. Somewhere, perhaps deep in Peter's soul, that thrill trembled but as far as his features showed, there was no lyrical emotion stirring him.

He looked down into the valley far away to where the Dee river flowed. Crops were doing especially well. He was doing tremendously well. And yet—— just as he was beginning to see a great future as it unfolded for him in the past—— the other end of that future, like a scorpion's tail began to curl up and make him troubled.

His wife was walking slowly through the yard about to shut in the hens. Since marrying her he had paid her little attention. He was not interested in her. She wearied him, but he was not going to let anyone know that. There were several who knew too much of his business—— the postmaster for instance—— but that in itself was not the cause of his concern. He wasn't certain what it was.

With his hands stiff by his sides and an expressionless face he looked remarkably like Captain Ahab in **Moby Dick** as he walked along that headland of potato drills. He was the man with the mad kink of resolution in him. It was a resolution every bit as insane as the pursuit of the white whale—— his resolution was to become the richest man in the whole country. His plan was to aim so very high that there would never come a day when his aim would be achieved and he might be forced to look backwards on his past.

Echoing through the valley the sound of crow-bar on stone was music in his ears. The work was going on, rolling on, and it would be about as much as he would be able to do to stop it now even if he tried.

CHAPTER 11

"Nothing thought of me, nothing thought of me," Mrs. Devine was saying as she sat by the fire that night attending to the pot of porridge.

Peter, reading **The Budget** listened patiently to her and then completely ignored her complaint.

She continued: "Boss everybody! would throw me out on the street, put me in the poorhouse."

At this moment Jemmy Pepper came in with the horses' collars on his shoulders which he hung on the peg in the corner near the fire. Seeing how matters were he again showed his fidelity to his master but in a foolish manner. Acting proxy for a man has its limits especially when he is a married man. And to assume the part of the husband, supporting him in a squabble with the wife, was going too far.

"How can the dacent man read the paper and you growling there all the time. Oughtn't you to have some sense?"

In a second that heap of spineless flesh came to violent life.

"Arra what? arra what?" she screamed the most appalling scream that Jemmy had ever heard—— and he had as he admitted afterwards, seen two women lunatics in his time.

In the silence that followed the scream there came from upstairs the sound of an old man's laugh. Old John knew his daughter. Immediately he had opened his mouth Jemmy realised that in doing so he had started something he couldn't stop. He was unacquainted with woman in a temper.

She seized the pot of gruel from the fire and flung the boiling stuff through the front window, clean through glass and casement. She screamed again and, if anything, her second outburst was more terrifying than the first. She threw herself on the kitchen floor and beat her head against the cement. She tore her hair.

Jemmy wept and said everything he could think of that might be soothing but he might as well be talking to a lunatic elephant.

He kept saying: "You're a good woman and I always knew you were a good woman. Good woman, good woman, good woman."

She got up off the floor and ran outside where she began to cry and clap her hands in the moonlight.

"Uch, uch, uch." She clapped her hands plaintively. "Uch, uch, uch. Oh, the Lord look down on me this night if it isn't I who's the woman to be pitied."

Piercing through the silent night valleys and over the hills the meaning of her words could not be gathered.

The neighbours within hearing distance gathered in their door-ways. Men who were brave in matters of this kind called their womenfolk to the door to hear the banshee. The shoemaker had visitors that night. In his matter-of-course way he was explaining to them all about the banshee. "She's come for John McKenna," he said, "she always cries for that party. Listen! Uch, uch, uch".

"Did you ever hear her before, Barney?" asked someone.

"Hear her!" he laughed; "I heard her a hundred times. Listen: uch, uch, uch...."

"Must be ould John" another remarked with open mouth.

"Take care," said another, "if it isn't the skilly-eyed one that he dumped in some workhouse. I bet it's her who is going to peg out."

So did they speculate. They were convinced of the banshee's reality and when a month later old John McKenna did die, they held Jemmy's tentative report on the truth as the last word in heresy.

In the meantime Peter's wife was still screaming in the street and Peter sitting bemused in a corner reading scandals out of the old newspaper. Suddenly he decided that the banshee had wailed enough. He got up, went into the street and dragged the wife into the house. Then grabbing a hames strap hanging over the fireplace he grabbed his wife around the waist with his left hand carrying out as he did so an upwards movement which lifted her skirts and petticoats behind so that her buttocks were exposed. Then he brought down the strap three times on the woman's bare behind. She quietened down at once and Peter went back to his news-paper.

ii

On Saturday when the men were being paid—— Jemmy had nine

shillings a week and the others seven each - Joe Toal noticed two sacks of potatoes leaning against the loft steps. He had a feeling that there was something special about them. He was correct, for the two bags of wizen potatoes were to be, this week, part of his wages—— the greater part.

There's two bags of spuds your mother asked me for," Peter said; "They'll let you have a couple of good eggs to go with them of a Sunday morning."

Joe Toal was raging mad but what could he do? His mother must have made the suggestion; she was another of those people who thought that money was a bad influence on a young fellow. And he wouldn't so much mind only he had planned to use some of the money to attend a football match the next day.

Peter and Jemmy Pepper went down the road together on the way to the pub to drink Jemmy's weekly wage.

The work went on. Work, work, work.

Joe Toal had several sisters. On Sunday morning Peter pulled up his side-car when passing Mrs. Toal and took her from amongst a crowd of other women—— considered a very mean act.

"Jump up, Mrs. Toal," he cried.

She was delighted to accept the offer of a man who appeared to be set for big things. She heard with disapproval the low deprecatory comments of the other women on Peter. "Hadn't a man with a yoke the right to give a lift to whomsoever he wished. Ha! the cheek of the beggars."

She sat beside Peter. The wife who was nearly as heavy as the two of them together was on the other side wearing her black sateen cloak and her usual bitter frown.

Peter spoke to Mrs. Toal in a low voice about that daughter of hers, "the gay one."

"She's a whipster, Peter; "begod that one does be heard where she isn't seen. Can't keep her off the roads."

"Would you think of letting her come to work for me, Minny?"

"In troth, she'll go. O bad luck to her to hell but she'll go. What stiffness would she be at not to go? It's about time she did something for her keep, the tinker. When would you be wanting her to come, Peter?"

"As soon as she can."

"That'll be the morrow morning and no later." The woman's voice fell to a secret whisper: "Herself is expecting....?"

"July," said Peter.

"Ah, a nice time of year when the milk 'll be plentiful and the weather warm." the speaker nodded sagely.

They pulled up at the forge door and the blacksmith's son tied the horse reins to the ring in the wall. On hearing Peter's car arrive the blacksmith came to the forge door and hung around speaking humbly to the woman. The shoemaker dropped the foot that he was measuring and spoke in a whisper to Peter.

"Of course she'll get it and welcome. Why wouldn't the poor woman get the turnip barrow to sow her turnips. To be sure she'll get it."

Peter went towards the chapel followed closely by the blacksmith. Mrs. Devine stayed behind for a moment to talk to the shoemaker.

"She will not get the turnip-barrow, so she won't," she said sourly. "It's not going to be lent that easy. How soft you must think we are!"

"That will be alright, Mary; that'll be alright."

"Well, make sure it will—— whoever she is."

She then followed her husband up the incline in the chapel. He was standing talking to the blacksmith. The blacksmith, who could drink as much as ten men wouldn't earn, was getting an advance on earnings from Peter —— five shillings. That, thought Peter, was a good investment.

Peter went to the belfry because Mass was already in progress when he arrived and he abhorred making himself conspicuous by marching in to the body of the church with everyone looking at him. On the other hand, he disliked being in the belfry among the roughs, the toughs, the poor of his native district and the politicians such as the shoemaker who since the anti-clerical row over Parnell, as a protest, never went inside the chapel during Mass. Through holes in the partition they could see into the chapel and, notwithstanding their irreverent attitudes, some of them prayed as fervently as contemplative nuns motionless at the foot of an altar.

Peter read his prayers out of a large grimy prayer-book that had a brass clasp and a corrugated spine. He looked as sourly pious as he could and some of his old companions who never grew up, and who cannot understand that some men do grow up and change, were doing their utmost to tear the mask off his face by reminding him of his youthful escapades.

The rue of Peter's visage increased in darkness. He never spoke a word or turned round to see who were the latest arrivals.

CHAPTER 12

In June old John McKenna died. After the screeching of the banshee everyone in Ballyrush expected a death. And all Peter's ill-wishers also expected that a death in the family would be followed by losses among the stock. They were surprised when this superstition did not prove true in this instance.

When the old man was buried Peter was very happy, so happy that he actually almost got really drunk. So nearly drunk was he that instead of pretending to be drunk–– his usual style–– he was on this occasion pretending to be sober.

The wheel of the year turned slowly, unexcitedly around. Peter's crops were, according to Jemmy who did Peter's boasting for him, the best in the parish.

"Oats! You wouldn't call that mist up there a crop of oats," he said to a neighbour one evening. "If you saw our oats! A total dread! Six feet tall–– I can't be seen walking through it–– and a shocking great colour too. There's grain half-way down the stalk."

"Yous 'll make a stack of money."

"And our praties," Jemmy went on hurriedly, "heads a dread to the living world!"

"Yous must have shoved on the nitrate of soda."

"Curse o' God on the ha'porth; only the dung. Ah, they may all say this and that and the other, but a good graipful of hen dung is worth all the nitrate of soda that ever was made. We have a piece of turnips and, honest to God, I never saw such mollockers. Big as a four-gallon pot. Pon my sowl."

"It's well to be yous, Jemmy."

In July Peter became the father of a girl. On the night of the birth Peter sent Teasy Toal, "the gay one" home. He had been employing her by the day for about a month and she was now getting a bit too familiar. In addition, she had the habit of bringing her mother and her seven sisters to Peter's house, as often as she got the chance, for a sup of tay. Peter knew for certain that on an occasion such as this when everyone who got the slightest chance would go mad with excitement at his expense, Teasy and her mother and all members of her family including relatives, would land in on top of them and eat and drink till they'd be ready to burst.

Peter had a professional midwife to attend to his wife, not because he thought a professional any better than a "handy-woman" such as Maggy Stanley, but because she would be the cheapest in the long run. A handy-woman, or a handy-man for that matter, who came for a "Thank you" always were the most costly in the long run. A man never had them paid.

On their way to the christening and passing Stanley's Cross Peter drove fast hoping that he would get by unknown to Maggy. But as he flew past he heard an unusually loud, sneering, laughing voice speaking to someone in Maggy's open doorway:

"A pratie-washer, I believe. Oh the devil in hell much loss. Thanks be to God that's one thing even Peter can't do—— have a son when he wants."

"What's that you said?" young Brigid called.

"I said there's a new pratie-washer arrived at Devines. He has a young daughter."

Maggy and her daughter laughed, a loud forced laugh that pursued Peter down the road for two hundred or more yards.

"There's nothing like a trained woman," Peter said to the midwife who was riding along with the baby on her knee. "There's a stob up there, Maggy Stanley, and I wouldn't let her attend an animal."

They met the shoemaker at the chapel door; he had come to stand as godfather to the infant. The midwife would be the godmother. After the ceremony Peter paid the priest the usual fee of two shillings. The godmother, not knowing of this and following custom, also offered to pay. Peter who had been standing aside rushed through the outstretched hands of the priest and the midwife brushing them aside. It was a very embarrassing situation. When the mind decides on doing something it often takes time to adjust itself to a contrary decision imposed upon it by outside circumstances. There was the priest jabbing away and the midwife jabbing away in an attempt to make connections between their hands. The priest was upset and didn't know quite what to do.

On the way down the path from the chapel, the shoemaker

caught up with Peter and the others. "You did what was properly right," he said, "too much money these priests have."

They went into Daly's pub.

"A pity it wasn't Father Hanratty," the shoemaker said as he drank his pint. "I'll never forget the time he tackled me—— the time I burned the anti-Parnellite papers outside the chapel gate. 'Ah, you low mane dog,' says he at the tip-top of his voice—— 'to make a show of me before the crowd going up to Mass.' 'Ah, you low mane dog,' says he 'why don't you be like any honest man and go and get married?' I was of course single at the time.

"And says I back to him in front of everyone at the top of my voice, 'Father, why don't you get married yourself? You're the only man that I know in the parish that can afford to keep a woman for there's not a loose shilling comes into the parish you don't get your hands on.' I tell you, he never tackled me again."

Peter was getting drunk: his eyes were bleary and the drop from his nose was more nauseating than usual. He was bitter and silent.

"You must go home with the child," said the midwife.

Peter never stirred. He sat looking at the rim of his glasses which hung between his knees, thinking far into the future—— or into the past.

Something was troubling him: anyone could sense that.

ii

At every opportunity—— which was seldom—— Mrs. Devine showed her authority. Peter was a "good man for a lend" but whenever the borrower arrived and Peter was out, the wife told them where they got off. She hardly ever spoke directly choosing rather to speak in grumpy asides:

"Half of the beggars of the country coming here for everything. If it's not a spade, it's a fork or a graip. That man is too soft; he doesn't know the beggars the way I know them."

"He said I'd find it in the open shed behind the winnowing machine and I just said I'd tell you."

"Yous know more about our things than the people that owns them," she whined. "Teasy, what are you doing there at the glass press?"

She spoke to the servant girl about this high-class piece of furniture, for the benefit of the neighbour at the door. Since they got the glass press and dumped the dresser in the barn Mrs. Devine drew it into every conversation by the skin of its teeth. Between the glass press and the fifteen cattle stable she had plenty of material for boasting purposes. Now Peter was to supply her with more. He bought a bull in addition to the boar he had for service.

No bull ever equalled the bull her father owned. He was the right sort of white with a yellow hide. There never was a white calf out of him. But half the people never paid up. Go to another bull the next year and if they met a person in fair or in market they'd hardly as much as look at you.

It was the second year of their marriage. The time was spring and in the fields the men were sowing and ploughing. Evening came on and Peter's men filled every crevice in the day with some job or other. The avenue was almost completed. The plan was such that improvements could always be made. The bottomless swamps on both sides of it were filled with rough stones. Poplar trees were being planted alongside.

The bushy fairy rocks were disappearing from the fields but there was still plenty remaining. Generations of superstitions had accumulated as insane notions accumulate in a man's mind.

The harvest came in. Peter dropped all superstitions about the harvest: he even reaped in the rain. Over on the scraggy hills of Drummas the scythemen would drop their tools at the slightest sign of wet weather.

It would be hard to find at this time of his life a more disagreeable or vicious looking person than Peter Devine. Barney Conlon, Maggy Stanley and Joe Toal all hated him and at the same time they couldn't help but be interested. Each one of them was making guesses at the nature of his secret self and trying to probe through the veil of mystery to the secret of his life in England. But he remained an enigma.

Walking along a headland, sticking his fist into the hearts of sheaves to see if they were yet dry he looked like a man who did not see beyond those fields.

He was getting richer. It was said—— and said correctly—— that he had loaned money to the man who owned the corn-mill in Ballyrush. He also loaned money to Joe Toal when their horse died and he had a mortgage on a little field they owned which was adjacent to his avenue. The blacksmith also owed him money but did not know how much he owed. Peter pretended he held no accurate accounting of the debt.

He was now three years married and a second child was born—— this time a son—— whom they christened Peter.

They sold the stud boar, Peter suddenly discovering after the sale that he was the worst animal that ever had been inflicted on a pig-producing country.

Then they sold the bull and bought another. Once more the bull they sold was in the words of Jemmy. "A narrow-gutted article that done a lot of harm. Only we found him out in time he would have destroyed the country." The new bull, was of course, a powerful beast.

CHAPTER 13

One December day Peter decided that he would go to the town of Dundalk with a load of hay for the military barracks. Peter, as far as possible, did all the marketing himself. As was the custom when dealing with English hay-buyers, he had the usual three loose axles and several half-hundred-weights hung beneath the cart. These would be weighed with the load and then disconnected when the empty cart was being weighed. One would need to look respectable for this trick to succeed. Peter knew that he was one of those serious-faced rogues whom nobody would suspect. Joe Toal's father had been caught in this fraud on an occasion and since then dared not show his face in the most fruitful hay-market in the country. It was a big loss to the man.

Peter went off to the town that morning sitting on top of the load and getting as near as ever he got to being excited by the poetry of the frosty morning fields. Jemmy took a short-cut and met him on the main road. He carried on his back a sack of good green unscutched hay which was to be for the horse's dinner.

Coming down the main road Peter had heard one of Toal's cows bawling and a thought flashed across his mind.

"Would you like to go with this load of hay? Jemmy,"

Jemmy jumped at the chance. Romance, magic—— all that was the town—— thrilled the dejected labouring man. He could scarcely believe his ears. Had he known what was ahead he would not have been so delighted.

Peter returned home. It was still not daylight and the stars and moon were yet in the sky. He remained indoors reading The Budget.

About eleven o'clock in the forenoon he slipped down to the field where the bull was grazing and as he approached the gate he sensed, without actually seeing, that someone was on the far side of the fence. Sure enough, as he suspected, there was Joe Toal and his father with their cow. Peter stole up the lane and stood silently in the gateway looking on. He stood there for the best part of twenty minutes and knew that though he had not yet been seen, his influence was being felt. To be watched doing something not quite right is to have a second conscience burning into one's mind. Although what they were doing was only saving a shilling and six-pence service fee, when they realised that they had been found out they almost fainted. Peter still said not a word. But his quiet stare--that was almost a smile—— had an insanity-making power. The gate was opened and the cow ran out. Peter caught the bull by the ring and the two men sidled away utterly abashed.

On that day, too, for no reason in the world, Peter's wife had another of her actress fits. When Peter and the other men came in for dinner they found the house in a dreadful condition. Pots and pans were lying around broken, water flowing over the floor and even the glass press broken. It was the broken glass-press that made Peter realise how terrible must have been his wife's temper--the one piece of furniture that distinguished their house from that of the neighbours who still cling to the old-fashioned dressers.

The servant girl was going about her work more cheerfully than ever. From the room behind the fire came the crying voice of the wife: "To think that any whipster could come in here and carry-on with a person's man. Oh, that the devil may take her and that's my prayer."

This was one of the few occasions when Peter was surprised. There was nothing that went before, no hint that the woman had a jealous mind. Would she be a bit touched? What was he to do in this situation? He thought a moment. Then he called her up from the room, speaking in the thinnest weasel-voiced squeal. Terrifying. "Mary," he addressed her, "give me down that ash-plant that's over the fireplace."

Trembling, she complied.

"Turn around." Then in the presence of the maid he administered six or seven sharp cutting blows on her behind. Administered is the correct word, for there was something coldly judicial about his manner. Mary quietened down.

91

The day passed and the evening came on and still no sign of Jemmy Pepper returning from the town. Peter was getting anxious. He went up the loft steps and stared and listened. There were carts rolling along the road in the distance but not his cart; he couldn't mistake the roll of his own cart's axle. It was not till one of the Kenny's of Drumbee, returning from his work in the Railroad Works, made his way to Devine's and told the story of Jemmy's mishap. Jemmy had been arrested for having attempted the fraud of extra weight of axles and ouncels on the soldiers.

"And is he in jail?" Peter asked.

"No", said the man, "as far as I have heard he got leave to bring home the horse and cart. He got out on bail, I think."

Jemmy arrived home around nine that evening. On being questioned it turned out that once again Jemmy proved himself a faithful servant. He denied to the police that his boss knew of the attempted fraud; and the police who knew of Peter as a "highly respectable farmer" believed him.

The incident disturbed Peter. There would be a court case and there is no telling what would come out in the open. It was the shoemaker who suggested to Peter that they should stage a rehearsal of the coming trial as the Kenny's were supposed to do. It was reported by a man, not a particular friend of the Kenny's that every time they had a court case coming up—— which was often enough owing to the number of crooked horses they gave warranties with—— they held a mock trial in their own house. The old father would be the judge and the mother and seven sons and two daughters would constitute the court, witnesses, lawyers and all. In that mock court according to the report of this man, the skin was perfected on many a far-fetched lie. Be this as it may, the Kennys were very successful in their law-suits, for the father went very hard against his own side and unless he gave a favourable decision they seldom went ahead with the case.

The shoemaker Conlon never had gone in for this sort of business before; he preferred soft talk, somewhat pious, and quiet intrusion on the other person's private affairs. He now thought that the staging of such a mock trial would add to this reputation. The idea oddly enough appealed to Peter Devine. It had in it an element of the practical joke which recalled his own boyhood.

Scene: The Shoemaker's Shop

Shoemaker: The defendant is charged with attempted fraud on horses of the English army. Do you plead guilty or not guilty?

Jemmy: Not guilty.

Shoemaker: Are you legally represented?

Jemmy: Eh?

Shoemaker: Have you a solicitor? (Looking around) Pat McArdle you take this man's case. Wait till we see. Who'll be the prosecuting solicitor? Come on, Tom Duffy, you ought to know plenty about the law and all the times you sat on a jury.

Tom: Right-o.

Shoemaker: Now we're all set. Let's open the case.

Tom Duffy: Your Honour, this is one of the worst cases that has ever come my way. It is the case of a poor ignorant labouring man who was sent out to rob and plunder by one of greatest scamps that ever walked on two feet. This mean low dog is called Peter Devine. He never was known to have done a decent act in his life. Since a yard made a coat for him he was a mean pup. Just because he happened to meet a slob of a woman with a farm, yous all think him somebody. Yous all think he has something good in him just because he happens to have a few pounds. Take a good look at the half-jack, Jemmy Pepper that's so ignorant it's as much as he'd know when he'd have his fill ate. He hasn't the cutting-up of a dog in him or he wouldn't walk the same side of the road as Peter Devine. He's a poor man, and a low man, and he's no man.

Peter Devine went to England and came back with three-hundred pounds to his name. Where did he get that money? Nobody knows, and yous all know that to know where a man gets his money from is to know all about him. I was in England but did I make three-hundred ha'pence? I did in me arse. But this weasel-faced thing with as much brains in his head as a sparrow, he can....

Peter: (in a temper) Barney?

Shoemaker: Address me as Your Worship, Peter.

Peter: Your Worship bedamned and double damned. This kind of scandalising is not good enough. Who is this Duffy?

Tom Duffy: Aw, didn't I know your oul' father that bought buck goats?

Peter: (Having his genealogy read, is staggered, brought back to his humble childhood. He loses all the silent power which he has shown during his married life and begins to talk volubly) And did I not know **your** father that had to have a collection made for him to buy a cow? Arra damn your sowl, what talk at yeh? Sure the half of yous wouldn't know how to spend money if yous had it. Arra, holy God—— sure yous wouldn't make a patch on a good man's trousers, some of yous. To hell with the court.

Cobbler: Order in the court!

Peter: Order bedamned!

Jemmy: To hell with the court!

Cobbler: You'll both be sorry for this. The thing is only a rehearsal. I want to hear evidence.

(Peter and Jemmy sit away from the ring which is the court and begin colloguing among themselves)

Tom Duffy: He's the lowest pig that ever walked on two feet.

Peter (to Jemmy): Are you coming?

Jemmy: I think we should wait to see how it goes.

Cobbler: It's a shameful thing that we shouldn't be able to sit here in peace and amity and try our own cases. No wonder the English try to make out that we can't govern ourselves.

Tom Duffy: Sure I knew his oul' father as well as I know myself. A little humpy fellow that some crow dropped from the sky, from the Lord knows where. Huh! wouldn't a person be the right bleddy cod to give any heed to a son of that thing. Then he goes to England and comes back with three hundred. Where did he get that only by plundering? He robbed a bank or something.

Peter: The devil thank you and thump you. Listen Cobbler, what's your verdict?

Cobbler: How can I give a verdict without hearing the evidence first? Come on and give evidence someone. Come on you, Joe, and act the soldier that found the axles under the load.

Joe: I found the axles under the load.

Cobbler: Go on.

Joe: That's all.

Cobbler: There should be more. Didn't you hand him over to the custody of the police?

Joe: I suppose I did.

Peter (interested; retreats from the doorway and returns to the ring): There were no axles under the load when the cart left my yard this morning, Your Worship.

Cobbler: Was there no axle in the cart? (Laughter)

Jemmy: The best axle in your country, a powerful axle.

Cobbler: (to Jemmy) How did these axles and ouncels come to be underneath the cart when the hay was a-weighing and not under it when the empty cart was put on the weighbridge?

Jemmy: I was bringing them in to have them fixed in the foundry.

Cobbler: (appreciatively) That's a good answer. Who owned them if they did not belong to Peter Devine?

Jemmy: A man that lives along the road to the town.

Cobbler: Do you know this man? Would you recognise him if you saw him? Why is he not in court?

Jemmy: (No answer).

Cobbler: I'm afraid it is going to be my painful duty to find this case proven. It is a bad case and the least sentence I can impose will be three months hard labour.

The court broke up: "I think we made a good job of it," said the shoemaker. He turned to Peter: "I don't think this case should be fought. You have no case."

Peter's blood was up. The mention of his father had stripped away the veneer and left him weak. "Sure didn't I know his ould father" was sufficient to reduce the proudest poetic pose to the level of the most unfortunate serf's. Peter was so shocked, so smashed that he could not realise the extraordinariness of Duffy's outburst. This man had known him too intimately.

When the case did come off it followed fairly closely on the lines of the mock trial. The verdict was a month in jail for Jemmy with the option of a fine of five pounds. Jemmy wanted to do the jail term but Peter, recovered from the coward-making remarks of Tom Duffy, calculated that Jemmy would be worth more to him than the five pounds at that time of year. So he paid the fine.

Being life and not art, Peter's career had in it no romantic progression. Day followed day in dull order and the light of the imagination fell on petty events as it has a habit of doing. And these petty events are in the end the only really important ones.

ii

Ever since the day when his origins had been mentioned by

Tom Duffy, Peter's cold, calculating power was losing ground to his imagination. The light of that imagination once made him very happy. In the green field before the house he saw his children playing in the sun and as he watched them he shared their delight in simple things. In the clods of dry earth under which they found, not worms and ants, but the tablets upon which the gods of poetry scratch the truths of the earth.

Turn but a stone and there am I

The children were strong and healthy; they were something new that had come suddenly into his thoughts—— making him afraid. But not for long.

Another few days had gone down the sink of time.

"Take them pair of mallets and break the lumps in the potatoes".

Jemmy was surprised by the manner in which the order was given. He expected a sign and nothing more. Peter was becoming human.

Since he had become humanised things were not going well with him either. The week before a cow had died while calving and his sow had a litter of only one. That was a bad sign. But Peter buried the cow publicly; he was not going to follow the pishrogues of some old woman on this matter.

The old women talked and the young women talked. The shoe-maker talked. Each of them saw in the omens a different nemesis.

"I'll bet you he'll cut down no more of those bushes."

"I'd rather he'd do it than me."

"They may all say this-and-that-and-the-other but the man that cuts them class of bushes doesn't make much out of it. Do you remember Bob Thompson the time he closed the cave on the big fort. If he had it to do again he wouldn't do it so quick."

That was the way the older people talked. The younger ones were inclined to blame his ill-luck on his dealings with Rosie Malone: "The man that laid heavy hands on a girl that way couldn't have a day's luck unless there was no God. A person wouldn't be safe walking the roads with a fellow like that on the go."

The shoemaker laughed at all these suggestions in an attempt to give the impression that only he knew. Knowing nothing he was able to give the idea of one who knew. There is nothing so profound and so puzzling as the shallows. Observers are always seeing more than is implied. As yet nothing worth speaking of had upset the steady course of Peter's climb. But simple folk can hear the flitting wings of Fate as it hovers close at hand. Fate was close at hand.

As the story shaped itself afterwards in the minds and imagination of the folk it took on a terrible symbolism. Peter, coming from the fair of Cross, was attacked at the dark corner of the road beside Thompson's front gate. His attacker was not a man or a woman or a beast—— it was none other than the Devil.

The marks that a man inflicts on a fellow creature are usually curable wounds of the flesh; the wounds inflicted by women are in nearly all cases curable by other women, but the marks inflicted by the devil are on the mind—— the external wounds being mere symbols.

On that night the moon was shining brightly and it was midsummer. Everyone agreed that it could have been nothing "right" that attacked Peter. When he was found the next morning lying in the water-table his face was contorted and his eyes were standing out of his head and his legs were paralysed. He could only speak in a stutter, he who had been such a mimicker of stammerers. Bodily injuries he had none except for a slight scratch on the face.

As soon as Barney Conlon heard of the affair he hot-footed it out to Devines, full of enthusiasm and that maudlin piety which oils the secret doors of an unfortunate heart. Peter lay in bed. Barney went straight to his room and at once got to work on the patient. Where did he meet the thing? What was it like? and many other of the childish questions that sick people have to tolerate.

"Peter," he whispered, "you didn't happen to do anything out-of-the-way when you were in Leeds?"

Peter shook his head.

Coming back from the room it gave the shoemaker a great deal of pleasure to reply to the wife's question: "How is he?" by the soft sympathetic hint given with a nod of the head: "I'd have a good eye kept on him if I were you."

That observation covered both a forecast of recovery or of death. The shoemaker was satisfied with his performance.

Down the lane he met Mrs. Toal who was coming to see the patient. "How are they all up there?" she asked.

"He won't pass this week" Barney replied with mighty satisfaction and expert finality.

"Oh may the Lord have mercy on him. A person should never be done thanking God for their health. And you tell me that? And what would be the matter with him, Barney?"

"He has a devil in him, Father Brady tells me. I met Father Brady yesterday and says I to him—— Lord, isn't he a very nice class of gentleman?"

"Terrible nice, Barney."

"Father, says I, would there be any truth in the story about Peter Devine being possessed by the devil?"

"That'll do you now, says he back to me; he has not one but a pair of the worst devils in hell jumping up and down inside him."

"Lord O Lord, Barney!"

The eyes of Barney and Mrs. Toal jumped with joy at the thought.

Shortly afterwards Mrs. Toal went into Devine's house and in a banshee wail offered her sympathy. The doctors had given Peter up and the parish priest had anointed him. Mrs. Devine began to see the horrible situation she was in—— a mother with four small children living on a hilly farm. What good would she be working the land? The crowd of neighbours would rob her if only for the pleasure of later giving her charity. They had never in their life needed charity and hoped that time would never come. She prayed, her children gathered around her.

It was not Barney Conlon who had first thought of Father Martin, the young priest—— though he claimed that honour. It was Mrs. Devine's own idea. He was a young priest who lived on the far side of the parish. He had been suspended for something serious and his mind was not perfect. He was reputed among the market women who went to Dundalk every Monday, to have power.

He visited Peter. He prayed at his bedside till the sweat flowed down his face. Sweat and blood, it was later said. He sprinkled Holy Water. He was performing one of those terrifying rituals of exorcism which are such an excitement in the imagination of country folk. What he did that evening would be talked about at crossroad, pub and fair for many a year to come.

CHAPTER 14

When Peter finally left his bed in September after three months illness he discovered that all Jemmy's enthusiasm was no substitute for his own supervision. Nor was Jemmy even worried. In spite of what pious people may say, no one in this world cares much about a man except his immediate relations. Outsiders, as Peter knew only too well, found their finest pleasure in another's misfortunes. Did't he himself?

Here were some of the losses during his illness: a mare worth forty pounds had died foaling; a cow fell in a bog-hole; the crows destroyed a field of turnips— and the worst of all bad signs— not one of his cows kept the bull. He gave in to the popular belief sufficiently not to disagree with those who consoled him by saying, "Something had to go."

During his convalescence Peter had a vision— not the usual sort of vision, but a vision nonetheless.

Planning ahead for his fields had been his diversion during his healthy days but while recovering from his illness he could not think of his fields so he thought of his children. He began with the eldest, Mary, and he followed her career far beyond the horizons of his knowledge. It was curious to find that the pattern of futurity worked out the same for a human being as for an inanimate field. He could prove nothing yet but he was sharp enough to note the pattern did not end in a knot. That proved to Peter the general design was correct. For three days and three nights he lay in bed trying to work out this mystery. He had followed his daughter's life till she was twelve years old. Then he began to get puzzled. She was going to be a lady. Education! That was the key. And the light that struck Saul as he went down the road to Damascus was no more marvellous revelation than this flash on the mind of Peter Devine.

Anyone who has ever been submerged in the unreasoning mud, a member of the doped uneducated classes, will understand how fantastic is the miracle that awakens a man. In all that country-side, in the whole parish of Ballyrush, which numbered more than a thousand families, there was not one who had ever dreamt of the world of education. There was, it is true, what was called tradi-tional learning and the love of learning but this was for the most part mere sentimentality. It was—— even when it repeated the old poems—— nothing better than the hunger for useless information which is satisfied by the popular press. The same was true of the hedge schools where pedantic Greek and Latin were taught parrot-like and in the same way the dictionary devoured. Joe Toal's father knew every word in Webster's Dictionary.

Peter saw a new light from where he was lying in the middle of a small farm. He saw that light go on until it illuminated a great city. He could see banks and hotels and government buildings. He could watch the secret society of the rich—— the really rich— and his own few pounds! How many had he? Four and five is nine and three is twelve. Sure that isn't money. His daughter Mary was sliding down that shaft of light to the city of banks and beauty. If she got there by whatever means was possible she could bring the other children after her. She must get there. He saw as he watched her being knocked down and degraded, and he saw her rise again and continue. He was tremendously excited. It was a race against time. Mary would have to be educated for the sake of the other children, especially the boys.

Peter kept this vision to himself and only hinted of it to his wife as a test to see if by chance she had seen the same light. She hadn't.

ii

"Jemmy!"

One word was enough. Peter was his old self again. The three workmen took the cue and were off to the rocks with picks and crowbars. Peter himself had to go to the village with the pony and cart for groceries. He also had to pick up the knives of the reaper from the blacksmith.

On that beautiful evening in August they cracked at the stones and slashed at the bushes. Jemmy grunted happily. Joe cursed savagely.

"What puzzles me," said he, "is why I stay working for this slave-driver."

"He's no slave-driver," Jemmy replied. He looked down the field. "There's the tay," he continued. "I said it before and I'll say it again, you're never hard-set till you have to keep the clock. The clock is the slaver."

They sat on stones drinking tea. The third man whom Peter had recently employed was another of those unfortunates of the tillage country, one of those thick-witted fellows who are never young and for whom Peter seemed to have a special attraction. Peter's place was in some ways like the Foreign Legion–– any-one, criminal, idiot or otherwise could get a start at Peter's. Tramps came to Peter and worked for nothing when they wouldn't go to a man who would be glad to have them and pay them.

Mat was one of these. He was a fellow with a large round head, a nose like the sock of an old swing-plough and–– not comparing the brute to the Christian–– he had a set of long teeth like the teeth of a horse. He and Jemmy were well met. Immediately they made each other's acquaintance they began to take a hand at each other as is the way with fools. One fool recognises another fool but not his own foolishness. To hear Mat talking you would think that the tribulations of twenty-five acres of watery soil were his.

But to continue like this might be to give the idea that there were no normal people in the parish of Ballyrush.

Ah, there are. See there beyond on the hill where Joe's eyes are turned, a boy and a girl looking for a quiet spot to sit down. Jemmy and Mat drinking the watery tea see nothing. Other people are to be seen. Coming round the turn in the distance at Thompson's gate are the two shop-girls who work in Dade's in the village. They are so beautiful, so unapproachable.

The parish priest walks slowly along the main Dundalk road near Stanley's Cross reading his Office and occasionally glancing over the fences enjoying the progress of the crops.

Two of the Kenny Brothers appear on the horizon driving before them a pair of head-hanging old horses.

Somewhere there is laughter of children. The thud-thud of a football being kicked was the drum joining in the symphony of the August evening.

iii

"It's about time Peter was back from the village." Jemmy was getting uneasy. Like Casabianca, the men remained at their posts because there was no Captain to give the order for dismissal. Darkness fell.

"I'm getting afraid," Joe said drolly.

"Who are you afraid of?" said Jemmy.

"Of ghosts."

The night fields sighed around them. The waving of the corn was like a lover's long gasp.

"Are we ever going to stop?" said Joe

"I suppose we are as well," Jemmy said.

The blackberries were ripening. It would be an early harvest. There were no briars now on Devine's side of the hedge but on the other side, in Toal's small meadow, they trailed several arches over the headland.

The workers went home.

Because he was three hours gone, the household began to get slightly anxious about Peter. The wife had been trained by him not to be anxious—— he kept her too much out of his councils for that. At last Peter arrived but without the cart. He was leading the pony who had shied and smashed the shafts of the cart. Peter had some poor body's blessing to come out so safe.

Another day dawned.

At the fair of Dundalk Barney Conlon, Maggy Stanley and Paddy McArdle were in a pub discussing in high spirits the downfall of Peter Devine. Their enjoyment took the usual form of enumerating and gloating over each individual misfortune. They searched their brains to root out very small item.

"The money won't be long slipping from him now," said Barney Conlon. He thumped the counter: "Isn't it the price of him? I say, isn't it the price of him? Sure the man wouldn't know there was a God if he were allowed to go on as he was."

Maggy heartily agreed. Paddy, a teetotaller, sober on lemonade, was also quietly pleased. The misfortune of a neighbour provided nearly all the best delights of that country. But they were not entirely correct about Peter. Peter was suffering losses but he still was making things pay. When the three people came out of the pub they ran straight into Peter. Barney Conlon, the shoemaker, rushed to him with all his maudlin sympathy.

"The dacentest man in the country," he shouted; "I know, for I was in with you on some of your biggest undertakings and we

102

know each other."

Peter was pretending to be drunk. He was in the process of making a deal with a long-nosed watery-faced Monaghan man who had a white calf for sale.

"How much?"

"Amn't I after telling you—— four pounds and not a penny less".

"Ten shillings a leg," offered Peter.

The seller to conceal the state of his mind swished his ash-plant in space and rushed around to the head of the calf to prevent other animals passing by from disturbing his little beast. He had been standing in the fair since morning and was going home in despair. No one had asked him what he was selling.

"Only I was scarce of grass I wouldn't have the calf here at all. I tell you, that's as good a wee sort as ever stood in this town."

"Did you rear it yourself?"

"I did," the man replied.

Mrs. Toal came on the scene. She too was pleased. They all felt that only Peter was hard-up he wouldn't be in the market for such poor stuff as this.

"Two pounds," Peter again offered.

"All up?"

"Aw, we'll have to get a drink out of it, anyway."

The calf became Peters at the price of two pounds. But that was not Peter's only purchase that day. The fair was one of the worst in living memory. Everyone wanted to sell and nobody wanted to buy except Peter. That was his policy. Even wise and crooked men looked upon this policy as stupid and a man like Peter as a fool even when he bought the stuff for half nothing.

It was on this day too that Peter bought the thoroughbred mare of the Kennys, they being absolutely certain that they had perpetrated one of the finest frauds of their career. They sold a beast that in their opinion wasn't worth five shillings a leg for six pounds. They were later to find out otherwise.

CHAPTER 15

The eldest of the Devine family, Mary, was not what one would call a beauty but she had her features and her health. A good, strong, healthy girl. "None of your fiddlesticks of things that a puff of smoke would blow away."

She wasn't particularly intelligent, though she had some of her father's cuteness. She was bold too, one who could give chin-wag to roadmen as she went to school. Her brother Paddy was like his father, a small, slight, thin-faced, pig-eyed chap who had the "dirty turn in him". At the age of six he could take the lynch-pin out of a man's cart or do any of the other practical jokes one finds in country places. More than anything else, he showed himself a true Devine in his cruelty to dogs of the neighbourhood who happened to straggle near Devine's house. Small dogs would be heard dashing away screaming.

They were sent to school every day: work around the house was never so urgent as to need their being kept at home. This was considered unusual in those days.

Mary was twelve. One evening when his wife was in good humour Peter mentioned that it would be a good idea to send Mary to the convent. This did not overly surprise Mrs. Devine. Many of the daughters of small farmers in the area had been sent to the convent for six weeks or less so they could have it to say they were convent educated. But Peter Devine had not this in mind and went on to explain.

"Beyond these beggarly fields was another world that laughed at our ha'pence. Somewhere over there...."

"But," the mother interposed.

"But nothing," he replied. "What I'm thinking about is to get her in, get her mixed up with the right people. She could be anything if she conducts herself."

Paddy was the mother's pet so the mother suggested that wouldn't it be wasting money on one that in the end would be getting married. "And what about Paddy?"

"That's the very thing I'm thinking about. If we can get Mary to go through the bushes in the gap all the others can follow."

"And what if they turn out like Henry McArdle?" the mother warned; "he was one of the smartest fellas in the whole country and as soon as he'd go in for an examination he'd forget everything. Wouldn't that be a poor look-out?"

Peter was willing to take that chance, so on the next fair day Peter called on the nuns and made arrangements for his daughter's education. She was to be a day boarder. At night she would lodge in Miss Campbell's, a well-known eating house in the vicinity of the sucker market. There was a swankier boarding-house down the street where children of solicitors, doctors and road surveyors lodged but Peter was a little shy of sending her there.

The sending of Mary Devine to the convent gave rise to many conversations. Maggy Stanley had the right good laugh. She told the shoemaker: "I met her last Monday week in the butter-market in Dundalk—— in the pick-market, good morrow to you—— she who was in the hurry. She had to get drawers for the young one, not one pair but two, one to wear while the other was a-washing. What do you think of that, Barney?

"These things have to be in it," Barney said philosophically. He ran his eye along the sole of a boot, "Yes, these things have to be in it, Maggy."

"And do you think they'll make anything out of her, Barney?"

"Arra, have a bit of gumption, woman—— not at all, as much chance as the big devil."

Both Barney Conlon and Maggy Stanley were as contented as two people who see a third invest in a lottery, fully satisfied that there is as good as no chance of winning.

Mrs. Devine had her own pleasures and one of the things that gave her most pleasure was not, oddly enough, boasting about Mary and the convent, but rather observing the discomfiture of the neighbours when occasionally they locked the gate on the avenue. Unless the gate were locked at least once a year a right-o'-way would be established. Knowledgeable people in the district claimed that having a lock hanging on the gate was enough. Mrs. Devine saw to it that this formal expression of private rights took place when somebody important was visiting the McArdles who normally used the avenue. Two daughters were nuns in

England and that very time were returning for a visit. Mrs. Devine saw to it that the gate was locked for their homecoming. It was also a source of great pleasure to see others trying the gate and having to turn back.

The new avenue created an incident which caused even more public diversion. In fact, it almost caused a local war. The people well-in the lane from Devines had threshed their corn with a flail since the days when flails were invented. Any day from October to March you could hear the thud of the flails on barn floors, or if the weather were fine, out in the open. Indeed, it was not until the arrival of the motor tractors in the 1930's that the old flail finally passed out of the lives of these people to become cobwebbed veiled mummies hanging from the collar-ties of lofts.

On this year Peter suggested to Henry Kerley who lived up the lane that he should have his corn threshed by machine rather than doing it by the flail. Peter promised to give the threshing mill passage across one of his fields. The two families who lived at the end of the lane were as shut off from civilization as a narrow lane could make them. The lane, however, which ran on to these isolated houses had to pass by Paddy McArdle's fields and was bounded on each side by them. There were no more civilized neighbours than the McArdles but the week or two before this incident one of the Kerleys had deliberately killed one of McArdle's ducks with a blow of a stone. And when Mrs. McArdle went to enquire about her duck the Kerleys made sneering remarks that annoyed the woman. Paddy McArdle would be a poor sort of man if he left that conduct off with them.

Chug, chug, chug. The huge engine passed over Devine's field and entered the narrow lane by the back of McArdle's house where the dunghill overflowed onto the lane. Jutting out from the wide clay fence at one point were three or four large boulders: unless these were removed the engine and thresher could never get by. And even if they did get by, further on was another narrow stretch of lane.

The Kerleys and the Kenneys (who were next-door neighbours) got their friends together and with crow-bars and pick-axes, spades and shovels, they cleared the road in front of the engine—— under a shower of stones and other missles. The machinery moved a perch or two before having to stop at more obstacles. This time McArdle re-inforcements had been brought up and the showers of stones drove off the road levellers. The machinery eventually had to stop where it was—— stuck in the lane unable to go backwards or forward. The battle lasted a fortnight and was only settled by the intervention of the parish priest, the curate and the police. The machinery was allowed through.

This was surely the happiest moment in Peter Devine's life; it awakened a boyhood nostalgia. In was the kind of situation he day-dreamed of years ago. Perhaps even now he had forseen the row when he encouraged the Kerleys to take the thresher.

Paddy Devine was sent to the same town as Mary to be educated by the Christian Brothers. The flag of Peter's hopes was now at the mast. The daughter was important but not for her own sake, only in so far as she could help the sons.

The boy went in and out to school on a bicycle each day but Mary came home only on weekends.

Mary was beginning to have a life of her own: she had become tired of her father and mother and their dirty ways.

She was also becoming quickly tired of the dirty lodging house in which she spent her nights. On fair days she walked the town, up and down the streets, hoping that some young lad might become interested in her. On such days she tried to avoid her father because he was always pretending to be drunk—— and her mother because of the habit she had of saying embarrassing things. She had no privacy while with the mother.

It was through her father she met Phil Ruddy. Phil was a man of about thirty-five, a solicitor without a practice whom Peter had once employed. The solicitor, Peter knew, had no money but he had something else of importance: he had the entrée to the best society. He knew the local doctor and veterinarian; he was often a visitor at Bolton's. Taking him all in all, he was a useful man to know. In addition Phil Ruddy had been in England and other distant parts. Unfortunately, money was the only wages of sin he didn't bring back with him. He was a low type and well-known among the girls as a man to avoid. He saw Mary every evening outside the town and when Mary came home on Saturday night her mother always asked her if she had seen Phil Ruddy. When she said she had the mother showed pleasure, thus leaving Mary at ease with her conscience.

Whatever could be said for Mary's intellect no word of praise could honestly be uttered on behalf of Paddy, the son. He was a bright lad in appearance as he cycled in and out of town. But it soon became apparent to the one or two intuitive critics of the parish—— those odd persons who speak wisdom unheeded—— that Paddy Devine was one of those bright, light-headed chaps who cannot be educated. So short a time do minds like his hold the impression that they remind one of a man trying to carry a lighted paper spill in windy weather across the fields to his house.

The father saw none of these defects. He was secretly more proud of the boy than his mother was. That boy, he promised himself, was going to be somebody. Peter, thrusting a pit of mangels at the back of the fence thought into the future. Things were becoming a little too like day-dreams and as soon as he realised this he set his will to work.

It was a wild windy day; a cold sleety rain slanted from the east. His two men were drawing home turnips. They were due now with the last load of the day. Here comes one cart—— young Joe Toal.

"Why didn't you fill the cart, Joe?" Peter asks without looking around.

"Who said I didn't fill it?" Joe replied as hurriedly he heeled up the cart into the shed.

The eye in the back of Peter's head was as keen as ever. He stood up and blew his nose. He stared in at the turnips in the shed. Joe, clambering over them at the rear of the heeled-up cart said in an off-hand way to Peter:

"I often wonder why you never went in for what the Cobbler Conlon calls public life. There must be something in it or all these other fellows wouldn't be so mad after it."

That actually was what Peter himself had been thinking. Strange, a man was never told anything until he first had thought it out for himself. It seems, we can only see in others what we already have discovered in ourselves.

ii

Joe Toal's young brother Sean was interested in Mary Devine. He was twenty and Mary fifteen. Walking home with her one evening he took his courage in his hands and decided to put his arm around the girl. He gathered up his courage. As soon as I count ten, I'll do it. He gripped her and then let her go. Then putting his hands deep in his trousers pockets, and his head high in the air, he continued walking beside her. She didn't jump, she didn't scream or laugh in that wild, noisy manner which is the country-girl's unpleasant method of self-protection. She was quite indifferent to what he considered was his terrible boldness.

Their love talk was the usual talk of sincere lovers anywhere. Always about other things.

"Man, that's a terrible fine evening," he said, his eyes wandering from hill to hill.

"A terror," was her reply.

"I say...." He stopped short and addressed the girl.

"Well?"

He made a wild gesture. "Oh, I only just thought of something, something not worth talking about."

The girl was puzzled. What was he trying to come at? Some men were like that—— they expected a girl to understand the secret thoughts that stopped short of their lips.

They walked through the hayfield by the hedge and through the gap out onto the lane above McArdles house. The scents of the summer night blended with the odours from the dunghill as they passed the house. The foliage of the whitethorn bushes was so heavy, the grass along the lane was so sensual—— the summer night was choked with beauty. The pale stars were in the sky. Three goats tethered to the stumps of bushes in the hedge carried their ropes across the lane.

They came to the gable of Devine's loft.

"Wait, Mary," the boy said.

"I'll have to go in, Sean."

"What hurry is on you? There's a thing I'd...."

The girl grasped one of the boy's wrists and held it tightly. She looked at him and he knew she had something to say. For no reason that he knew he rushed on to talk of all sorts of irrelevant things—— although he wanted to hear her story. It was a form of chivalry that was instinctive with him in other matters too. When anyone was about to tell him a secret, when after squeezing the secret to the very lips of its keeper, he would rush off and refuse to listen.

"Some day you will learn," she gasped and rushed off in the most theatrical manner.

She was always like that, always left him hanging in the air.

109

It was pleasant, lyrical, living in that country then. Everything was so simple, so uncomplex, so mediaeval. No motor lorries on the roads and only one motor car. Bicycles were only then becoming plentiful: none of the older people could ride one. And Maggy Stanley recounted the words of some prophesy which forecast that the public road would run through someone's kitchen and that the coach without a horse would go along the road. It came to pass.

But if these unimportant things were simple and old–fashioned, the inscrutable heart which is the same among kings as peasants made these lives complex and produced the truest tragedy. What have material events to do with tragedy!

Then, to walk along that Dundalk-Crossmaglen road of a Sunday between Masses in summer–– or when a soft rain was falling on the dust in the water-tables–– was to feel the old, the unchangeable, the fairylike land.

How fast the walkers on those roads travelled! Those were the days when a man or a woman took pride in their feet. Those were the days when a good pair of hand-made boots were necessary.

It had been thought that the Great War which raged for four years in Europe would change all this. There were changes but not all that many.

CHAPTER 16

It was a fine evening in the middle of the week. Peter was coming from the village where he had been speaking to the owner of the Ballyrush cornmill. He had as good as bought the mill. Now he was going in the direction of the shoemaker's to have a piece of harness repaired.

As he turned into the weedy, briary path to the house he came upon a cousin of the shoemaker coming out—— a cousin who lived in a distant town. He had heard Barney Conlon in bidding him good-bye say: "I think we should be able to work it for you if that other greedy...." At that moment Peter came into view and the sentence was unfinished.

Peter sat down in Barney Conlon's shop. In no time there were seven or eight visitors. The shoemaker took off his apron, shook it outside the door, and then sweeping all the scraps of leather into the fire he was ready to talk for the rest of the evening.

The conversation began gently flattering Peter. Wasn't he the good judge of horses. Remember that old "screw" he bought from the Kenny's which they thought was about to die and didn't Peter sell it two years later for a hundred pounds—— a real thoroughbred.

Gradually the conversation drifted towards the Ballyrush corn-mill.

"There was never any luck about that mill," said the shoemaker. "The man that had it before this fellow was drowned one winter's night in the tail-race—— and the horse and cart along with him. And the man who had it before him fared no better.

"He was a strange fellow, made himself a pair of wings and went on top of the mill one windy day to try them out. God be good to him; I well remember him though I was but a gassan at the time. It was of a February.

"There was always bad luck going with that mill. Paddy the kiln-man used to tell me stories that would put the hair standing on your head. About the time the dog—— it was nobody but the devil himself–– used to come every night when he'd be up minding the kiln, Every night the dog came and begod...."

"That's not the story at all," someone chimed in.

"Well, go on you and tell it."

"The kiln-man had no dog: he only used to hear something growling that sounded like a dog."

"You're right, you're right there," said the shoemaker. "That's how it was. So what did he do, only the next night he brought his own bulldog with him–– a shocking big bruiser of a baste.

"I remember him telling me the story. 'I was sitting,' says he, 'about twelve o'clock at night making myself a cup of tay on the ashes of the kiln fire. It was one of the finest nights I ever remember; you could lie out at the back of a ditch. There I was and the dog sitting beside me. Round about half-twelve the dog began to tremble and shake all over and begod,' says he, 'I knew that there had to be something curious about the affair. Begod,' says Paddy to me, 'I gave my dog a bit of courage and says to him "Go For Him, Mick."'

"That I may never tell a word of a lie on Paddy the kilnman that's dead these fifteen years, he told me that all that night, till three in the morning his bulldog fought a ghost. Fought the Devil. And Paddy saw nothing. There, the dog, his big bulldog, would lep into the air and scringe his teeth and snap and," the shoemaker brought his fist down on the edge of the bench, "there's men alive today who can tell you they saw that bulldog the next morning and you never saw such an unfortunate dog in all your life."

He glanced around the company avoiding Peter's eye as far as possible because he felt that talk of the Devil was not exactly Peter's happiest diversion.

Peter laughed when he might be expected to do the opposite. That was one of the worst features of life in a community such as this: effect did not follow cause. Life was a series of episodes.

The shoemaker continued talking about the mill. He recalled four generations of owners who were bankrupt by it. Another defect in the mill was the low water level in the spring and summer–sometimes even into the autumn.

"And does any of you remember the young one of Pat O'Brien–and a bloody fine girl she was–– that Pat used to have in the wee pub on the hill?", old Johnie Toal chimed in.

112

"What's this, now, that was?"

"She's the one that used to be the barmaid in the little pub on the hill above the mill. Died suddenly after some tinkers came that way one night—— and however they interfered with the unfortunate girl there was nobody to hear her screaming."

"That was a bad job, alright. That would be about the time Peter here was in England."

Peter was amused. He even joined in the yarns about the mill, for it wasn't the monetary value of the mill alone that interested Peter: no more than the next man, he did not live on bread alone. In possessing the Ballyrush mill with all its ghosts and legends he felt that he was joining a great family.

His immediate problem was to decide whether he should leave the home place and go and live in the village at the cornmill. There was a fine dwelling beside the mill, a wonderful old-fashioned house with passages that led through dark ways into gardens where wild woodbine was trellised around curved wooden arches instead of the rambling roses that used to grow there.

He had often been out in that garden behind the house, and the queer rancid smell was the smell peculiar to the backyards of houses of the gentry. Now that he analysed such smells that had come down to him from his childhood he realised that they were caused mostly by bad drains. The smell of old suds, old vegetables, blended with the scent of flowers or apple blossoms. The thoughts and smells of that mill-house were beautiful in his imagination.

And the path above the mill-race right beside the railway! There were a row of lead pipes laid along there but what they were for he never did know. His thoughts returned to the house, to the pump that pumped water up to the cistern on the roof, and to the unusual type of architecture. It was a three-storeyed house but the top storey was low, as in the houses built by the landlord's agents at one time. It would be nice to go up there of a summer's day and sit at the window from where he could see half of the parish.

Better than all was owning the mill. He liked people to hear people talking of its ghosts and devils. Besides, there had not been sold a house in that area without some story of ghosts and spirits.

The mill was very well, and the house that went with it wonderful, but most important of all was the education of his children.

Only on very few occasions in her life was Mrs. Devine called upon to make so difficult a decision as the one posed to her now by her husband. Not, it may be added, that her decision would make any difference. All depended on what Peter decided.

She considered and considered. There was the avenue and the locked gate and the delight it gave her watching the annoyance of the neighbours in finding it locked. There was the parlour with its "chairs to match and curtains to match." There was the fifteen-cattle stable. There was the turnip barrow. And above all there were the neighbours whom the woman loved because of the pleasure they gave her when she made them miserable.

Phil Ruddy who had given up going with Mary returned this very evening in the company of Mary's sister Jane who was now also going to the convent. This turn of events disturbed Mrs. Devine but the for moment she could not afford to think about it. It was Phil's opinion that it was essential they move to the mill-house. That would have settled it, had there been any need to settle it—— for Peter had already made the decision to move.

Everything, including the views of Peter and his wife and family, had to be changed now. Peter would have to stop walking with his hands clasped behind his back and a drop hanging from his nose. He would have to rise to the occasion. To change the outlook of the family was a problem. They had no idea how to behave in a large house, a house in which people of substance if not of quality had lived.

The necessary changes took place only on the surface of their lives but the underlying material remained substantially the same.

To be elected a member of the County Council was now a necessity. The last owner of the mill had been a member for twenty-two years and the man before that had, as the shoemaker pointed out, been a "prominent member of public boords." A curious reflection crossed Peter's mind: no father and son so far as was known had continued in ownership of the mill. It appeared that there was in fact some ghost which made ownership of the mill a life-interest only—— or even less.

CHAPTER 17

The local Elections took place the summer following Peter's arrival in the Mill House. Peter had never been a politician in the strict sense and this turned out to his advantage. He got the votes in the same way that other "responsible" candidates got them. On Sundays, after Mass, he would slip up behind a man and give him a tap on the shoulder and the man whose shoulder he had tapped would turn around and say: "That'll be alright." Peter was elected to the County Council.

He lived in the Mill House and was wondering what to do with his old house, now vacant, when a new schoolmaster came along and he rented it to him—— though he kept the farm. Running the farm and the mill did not strain Peter's capacity. Indeed, he still felt that a large part of his powers were idling. Bob Thompson, the Presbyterian neighbour, sold his farm shortly afterwards and Peter bought that too.

When people get rich they do not change so much as create change in others. Those very people who had known Peter as a boy changed their attitude. They kow-towed to him, and seeing him now through the profundities of money saw profundities of mind and moral qualities underneath. If one of them were asked what were Peter's roots they would feel tongue-tied. They could hardly recall.

Some of the old furniture of the farmhouse had been brought to the Mill House—— the best pieces of the parlour, the "chairs to match and the curtains to match" and the big gazetteer which completed the effect—— as it completed the effect in every country parlour—— was introduced. On Sundays at Mass Peter and his wife sat in the "men's seats." The sexes in Ballyrush parish were segregated on opposite sides of the centre aisle. Only the very important broke this tradition. On public collection days in the church when names of contributors were read out, they gave a pound when sixpence was the average.

Both daughters, Mary and Jane, were now entered in the convent as full time boarders. On fair days Mrs. Devine visited her daughters. On one of these occasions a too gentle nun whom Mrs. Devine did not like said to her:

"As you have a grand piano at home I thought it would be no more than right that Mary should learn to play it."

A grand piano! The Devines had no piano, grand or small but Mrs. Devine, having imbibed some of her husband's subtlety, sang dumb, admitting nothing. She also kept dark the fact that she had a poor opinion of musicians; to hear her talk they were no better than tramps. She had never known one that wasn't poor—and low, into the bargain. So as the saying goes, she took on with the grand piano and agreed to Mary's having the lessons.

Mrs. Devine had some money in her own name in the bank. For a few years back she had been holding on to the proceeds of eggs, fowl and butter without her husband's overt consent. She decided that before leaving the town she would look around for a piano and if she found one would pay for it from her own bank account.

She went in to Dick Coyle's which was a well-known junk shop as well as being one of those Rosary-hung establishments where, as the customer goes in, he is tickled by hundreds of Rosaries hung from the ceiling. It was in Coyle's that five years before Mrs. Devine had bought those six holy pictures that were hung in their bedroom and which were the talk of the country: "Cost fifteen shillings each—— the frames alone were worth the money."

When the woman heard the price he was asking for an old piano she nearly "foaled a fiddler" to use her own expression.

"Ten pounds!" she exclaimed, "Arra, Dick, dear, do you think me mad to give that much for a piano? Why that...."

"I could give you one at a cheaper rate, Mrs. Devine," said he, "but I couldn't recommend it."

Mrs. Devine bought the piano with great reluctance and Dick Coyle delivered it that same evening.

It took some time for Peter to get the measure of this new development correct in his mind but eventually he was satisfied that it was the right thing. His wife already had acclimatised herself to the idea and was even then beginning to wonder why they had not thought of a piano before.

The piano was put in a corner of the drawing room and upon it was placed a large vase of artificial flowers, Mrs. Devine remembering having seen such a bunch of flowers on a piano in the hotel in the town. Standing in the door of that room she was reasonably satisfied with the arrangement of the furniture and the quality of the decorations. As far as possible everything had been planned on the style of that hotel lounge.

On the walls were pictures—— also bought in Coyle's—— of highland cattle standing ankle-deep in a summer stream. Matching that picture on the opposite wall was a picture of a racehorse.

In the centre of the floor was a splendid round mahogany table with the big gazetteer for the year 1880 in the middle of it. The floor had a carpet that cost seven pounds. In a corner was a bookcase filled with books. These books had titles like **Leaves From a Journal of Our Life in the Highlands** by Queen Victoria. Mary had recommended this book to her mother when she saw it one day offered for sale by a seller of secondhand clothes on the Market Square. This particular purchase troubled Mrs. Devine's conscience more than anything else. If there was one thing she could see no use for it was books when they weren't schoolbooks. Imagine the idea of such a lot of books! But in time she got used to the idea and even recognised it as a necessary part of high-class life.

Being rich had its drawbacks, she discovered. The priest's housekeeper suggested to Mrs. Devine that they could do no better than invite the new curate to tea sometimes. So, on one evening in June the new curate walked up to Mill House to be entertained.

When Mrs. Devine opened the door to Father Brady she was opening a new door on her mind. For the first time in her life she was to become acquainted with the fact—— unknown in rural places—— that a priest is an ordinary man. Even mothers of priests are usually ignorant of the truth of their children whether they be saints or sinners.

She shook hands with the priest and welcomed him to their house. When she showed him to a chair in the drawing room she involuntarily made a swipe with her palm as if to wipe the dust—— or worse—— off the chair. Then she sat down before him and tried to feel at ease.

What would she talk about? She did not know what priests talk about. Just the same in no time at all she felt free if not quite easy. He looked around at the pictures on the wall and made a complimentary remark. They talked about the weather.

"Paddy will be coming home on holidays," said the priest.

"The week after next, Father. Indeed he sent for his train fare yesterday. I hope he's attending to his business and not wasting too much time on football. The same football was the misfortune of many a man."

"He's the best half-back in college, Mrs. Devine; you should be proud of him."

The priest lit a cigarette and leaned back in the horse-hair chair, puffing away.

"I was just wondering," said he, that your husband doesn't think of getting a motor car. He could get about to fairs and markets much quicker. I am thinking of getting one myself."

"But, sure, who'd drive?"

"Your husband could learn to drive. Easiest thing in the world."

Mrs. Devine did not take the suggestion of the car too seriously, else she would have been more shaken by it than she had been when the idea of the piano was first raised. Yet that casual remark turned out to have a good deal of bearing on Peter's subsequent fortunes.

Peter came into the room for a few minutes and the priest again referred to the car. He clapped his hands together gleefully like an undertaker during an influenza epidemic and showed some traces of hysteria.

"That's the very thing I was thinking of!" he said.

"The future of the country is in the motor car, Mr. Devine," said the priest? "and success consists in being able to see into the future. Railways will soon be a thing of the past."

The priest speculated on various possibilities in business development and Peter listened as though a thought concerning them had never entered his head. Actually, since coming into possession of the mill he had developed the distant-sight for agricultural affairs which he had already had, into a telescope which worked equally well for the larger world of commerce.

The shoemaker had been suggesting to him that he should buy railway shares and Peter listened pretending to agree. The gods bring thread to weave a web begun, the Sufi philosophy teaches, and almost everything Peter now saw gave him an idea. He seemed to possess that sense of life which is the greatest asset possessed by the Jews. He could sense a new vital growth in its earliest stages. Even as he gaped at the talkative young priest he became aware of another prospect. The priest had smoked three cigarettes since

118

coming into the room: a bit of money in a cigarette factory would be no dead loss, he thought. But he mentioned not a word about this.

The welfare of the parish was discussed and the priest thought that a new hall would be an inestimable benefit to the parish. Too many parishioners were leaving the village on Saturday nights for the town. Peter could see that a new hall was necessary even though he never stood inside such a place. It was the essential flippancy which takes the strain of business—— a diversion. He did not think of the matter in terms as lucid as this but he did think of it.

His wife was rising to the occasion in fine style. She ordered the maid to bring tea. Two of the children came in during the tea and Mrs. Devine had to make a grimace behind the priest's back to get them to leave. Later she had to endure her children's mimicry of her grimace—— for the children observed every affectation of their mother and took the utmost pleasure in making her uncomfortable for it.

There was a time when Mrs. Devine day-dreamed of the aristocratic life—— as many humble people do—— daydreaming that her great-great-great grandfathers were chieftains or at least schoolmasters. Didn't the cobbler claim that his great-grandfather was the owner of the place that was now the Glebe in Dunlay? Mrs. Devine's daydreams had injured rather than assisted her present actuality of life. She was half-way between the dream and the reality and that—— as everyone knows—— is the treacherous gap between the stools.

The priest departed, promising to call again soon.

CHAPTER 18

It would be hard to exaggerate the enormity of the struggle that went on in the minds of both Peter and his wife as they tried to sit at ease on the pedestal which Peter by his own skill had erected. Every morning he rose a peasant and every morning his wife automatically showed that personal restraint during her personal toilette that is the happy privilege of nobodies. It was always near dinnertime by the time they got the hang of it.

During the summer evenings Peter walked in the garden beside the river at the back of the house and there held commune with the spirits of wealth and influence who ask no questions as to a man's genealogy. There was an air about that garden. It had walks with box hedges and it had flowers and shrubs. The man who could stand or sit at the bottom of that garden of an evening in summer with the river murmuring gently behind him and all the jungle profusion of shrubs without becoming a poet would indeed have little virtue. It affected Peter without his being aware of it. But perhaps what affected him most was the backyard where the smell of stale suds remained in his memory as a phoenix eternally rising from the ash-pit.

He sniffed at the stagnant water in the trough underneath the pump and he sometimes turned up a loose flag-stone to revel in the aroma of rotting vegetation that came up.

During the day the rows of carts arrived and, unlike the previous owner of the mill who often had to send these customers home for lack of river water to turn the wheel, Peter was able to serve all — for he had installed a new patent turbine motor which worked in place of the water. Standing in the doorway of the third loft of the mill Peter often surveyed the rows of carts and, though it was a thing he would never dream of allowing anyone to suspect in him, he would laugh to himself at the thought of his being the owner of the mill—— he who as a boy had waited there in the queue of carts with the wind blowing through the torn seat of his pants.

Perhaps they weren't my worse days, either, he would muse. Perhaps. Then he would laugh again and, if someone backing a cart into the door underneath him chanced to look up, he put on his narrowest, bitterest growl and shouted at his men. Shouting was a practice he never believed in until he came to own the mill and found that the men there had been used to a shouter.

It is always illuminating to know how much money a man has. Find out where a man gets his livelihood, and how much it is, and you know more about his inner soul than the priest who hears his Confession. Peter's financial entanglements, as he called them, were so involved and extensive that an account of them would take up too much space in this narrative. Just a few additional examples will be given.

Before selling the old thoroughbred screw—— already mentioned—— he bred her and to the surprise of everyone she produced a foal. This foal formed the basis of a whole stable of racehorses and Peter found himself in the racehorse business. He foreclosed on several of his creditors and added more land to what he already owned. He bought and sold a local pub at an excessive profit—— to the dismay and destruction of the unfortunate Roscommon farmer who sank his life's savings in it. The buyer committed suicide.

He bought a lorry as well as a motor-car. He began to import Indian corn, grind it in his mill and deliver it with his lorry to the nearby towns—— the notorious "yallow male."

He kept a stallion at the old place.

His four children were being educated. Mary was at the university in Dublin, Paddy was at the seminary hoping to become a priest—— if nothing else—— while the other two, Jane and Henry were still in boarding school.

Peter Devine was now thoroughly respectable; his past was forgotten, or nearly so. Yet, there were problems.

One night the dead body of the postman Duffy was fished out of the river near the mill—— near a point where Peter had been seen the evening before talking to him. There was no suggestion among the police that Peter had anything to do with the death—— even though everyone in the countryside claimed to know the ins and outs of the case—— and the murder! In these conversations at firesides and cross-roads it was said that Tom Duffy had got some

121

new information about Peter's career in England, and it was the implied threat that caused Peter Devine to throw the postman in the river. But there was no real basis to this theory. Their argument got some psychological support three years later when Peter Devine, sitting on a jury in a case remarkably similar to this one–was the only man on the jury to vote for acquittal. The same defendant was found guilty at a subsequent trial.

But in spite of these rumours Peter went on to his destiny shoving aside such trifling annoyances.

CHAPTER 19

Mary had grown into a fine, if coarse girl. At the age of twenty she was attractive to countrymen who saw in her something beyond their reach. When she came home from the University for the summer holidays many a humble ploughman's heart offered her the secret rose of his love. In the chapel on Sundays men's eyes would be staring in her direction while pretending to be looking in another. When in the evenings she went out walking on the road with her mother or with her sister, poor men hurried to clean the dry clay off their boots and shave the stubble off their faces.

Yet not one of these lovers ever unfolded from the bud of his secret rose to make an approach to the girl. An approach would have been very welcome to her for up to now she had neither men friends nor lovers in the city. She looked too common in the city and too rare in the country. Not that she wasn't trying to achieve that dignity which is approachable, and that familiarity which is the balance of beauty. In her own way she was without success.

Now as she approached the age of thirty she developed into a tall yet stout person with a heavy face like her mother's. She had a large bosom and–– considering her height–– short legs. She had many of her mother's traits of character. She was capable of going into tantrums for no reason, she was easily insulted and she insulted back, she talked with a drawl and she had small feet.

Mother and daughter were walking out the road in the direction of Stanley's Cross on an evening in July that pulsated with the Spirit of Nature, the intangible spirit of beauty. In the green hedges the robins and sparrows chirruped and chirruped. Cows in corners of small fields stood dreamily chewing the cud after having been milked.

The evening road was empty except for a goat which was standing on its hind legs picking at the bark of a tree near Stanley's Cross. On the window-sills of houses in off the road they could see

123

men resting legs while they rubbed the clay off their trousers. Faces peeped at doors.

Mrs. Devine who had forgotten her handkerchief was waiting for a quiet leafy spot where she could blow her nose without being seen—— she was a rich woman now and for her to be seen blowing her nose into the grass margin would not be a lift to her dignity.

She had given a peep around. Nobody was looking. She blew her nose with great satisfaction. "Such a dirty woman," commented Mary as both of them put on very serious faces as if nothing shameful had occurred.

Father Brady was coming round the corner on his bicycle. He dismounted and the three of them had a long conversation on the road about one hundred yards from Stanley's Cross. Maggy Stanley noticing the confab stole along the hedge to be within earshot while at the same time preparing for a hasty retreat to a spot where it would seem she hadn't been listening.

The priest made a few jokes about city life. Mary wasn't too interested in getting a degree, she said.

"And how is Paddy getting along?"

They stood in on the grass margin to let a lorry pass. They all stared at it, for the lorry was a rare and awful contraption on those roads in those days. It had solid tires and its sideboards rattling made a noise like thunder.

"I don't know what kept Charlie with that yoke," said Mrs. Devine. The lorry was Peter's and was returning empty after a delivery to the neighbouring town of a load of Indian meal—— Injun Buck.

"Yes, Paddy. Oh, he's doing well but you know those Capuchins make a lad study. It will take a little time but with the grace of God all will be well."

Mrs. Devine went on to boast of her success so much so that the priest was inclined to retch at times at the obscene litany. But he remained at ease, experience having taught him that loving your enemies was not nearly as difficult or as chastening as loving those to whom you are indifferent. To be able to appreciate another man or woman's point of view, or their hearts, is to become wise. Another heart understood is another scalp added to the belt of the Indian Warrior of life that is in us.

Mary had affected an educated accent and it was the priest's explanation that she picked up the accent because she had a very keen ear for music. There were others who claimed that it was due to the absence of any standards of judgment.

Some months before this Mary had received a letter with the name **Devine** mis-typed to read *De Vine*. Mary jumped at the error and now had convinced her mother—— and her father—— to pronounce the name De-Van-eh in future and even put it in this form on all official billheads.

De-Vaan-eh, the mother kept repeating under her breath even during conversations.

After the priest had left their company Mrs. Devine again blew her nose. "I'll go home," said the daughter, "if you go on like that."

"Go home to hell if you like," the mother responded.

"Railly, Mother!"

Once again the power of Mary's accent recalled the woman to consciousness of her high place in society and she apologised for having forgotten her handkerchief. "Would you give me yours, Mary?"

Maggy Stanley had by now retreated to her own doorstep. She shouted down to the Devines: "Good evening, ladies."

"Good evening, Maggy," Mrs. Devine shouted back.

Mary was displeased with her mother.

"You shouldn't be shouting across fields like that: it is not respectable."

"Not worth being alive if a body can do nothing. I never saw one could bring back so many new-fangled notions from any place as you."

It was a great strain on Mrs. Devine to have to live up to her daughter's notions but, to give the woman credit, she was willing to try her very best even if she would lose a good deal of familiar happiness by doing so. The daughter had been at her since she had come home on holidays. The first days were the worst both from the point of view of the accent and the acquiring of new habits.

Mary had given up the idea of being a musician. She did not play the piano now, not that it could ever truthfully be said that she played it. The truth is that she hadn't the ghost of an ear for music. It was her younger sister Jane who now hammered away on that instrument.

Mary's new idea was to become an actress and unknown to her mother had already begun to take lessons in acting from a shady character who had a School of Acting in the city. She had many qualifications for an acting career–– she was superficial, she had an excess of stupid vanity–– and most of all–– she knew nothing and cared nothing about dramatic literature.

"I think the stage is wonderful" she told her mother just to see how she would react.

"What stage?" inquired the mother–– "Good evening Johnie, lovely weather–– What stage are you talking about?"

"The theatre–– acting in plays."

"What? Is it like Phil Gray that was around last week in Ballyrush with his face painted and his bad language. Sure, he's no better than a tinker. Is it going to join the gypsies you have in mind? That's odd and you with such high notions. I sometimes don't know what to make of you."

Mary was exasperated. She could explain nothing, not the simplest things to her mother.

"It's a very high profession in the city, mother; ladies and gentlemen go in for acting. You can understand nothing."

"Is there any rich man looking after you?" said the mother suddenly changing the conversation to something more practical, something she could understand. "–– Hello, James."

"My God, speaking to everyone you meet!"

"I can speak to whoever I like, Mary."

The mother's reply was not completely sincere believing that there may be something in her daughter's suggestion. She was sure of her ground only when the subject was men and in particular, men who were prospective husbands.

"It would be better, far better, for you to keep your eye open for a good man what would give you a good home than to be thinking of all these other notions."

Again Mary was exasperated. Could her mother not realise that nobody was trying harder than she to catch a rich or even moderately rich man for a husband. It was like driving a willing horse.

"The last time you were home you were talking about a fellow who was going to be a doctor and this time you haven't a word about him."

"Listen, mother," the girl said very emphatically, "didn't I tell you that I only met him once, casually, and that was all there was to it."

In her mind the mother was measuring up the pros and cons of the matter. Mary did say that she had got in with a young fellow, the son of a big shopkeeper, who was going to be a doctor. The story had given Mrs. Devine much pleasure and she had been looking forward to Mary's homecoming to inquire how the court-ship was progressing. In a mother's peculiar way she had been ex-tracting the evidence by what she considered to be well-chosen random questions and remarks.

"A doctor is a good trade."

"Indeed, it's not a good trade."

"And what is a good trade? Surely a solicitor is as good as a doctor?"

"An actor would make more than either."

So Mary was going about with an actor and she herself was thinking of becoming one too. At first when Mrs. Devine heard about the actor she regarded the idea as preposterous but if as Mary said respectable people (otherwise rich people) went in for acting she was willing to change her outlook. Mary might well be right and quickly she began to adjust to this view. "De Van-eh" she said, "it certainly sounds swanky." She determined to per-suade her correspondents to use this form of the name.

When mother and daughter arrived home after their walk Paddy was going out to kick football with the village boys. The mother was glad to see him go for she wanted him not to fail on his road to the priesthood and she knew that a man seldom failed on this road through dullness at books but through an attraction for girls. Kicking a football kept him from bad thoughts.

Paddy was unpopular among the boys with whom he played football. Like his eldest sister he had the unpleasant knack of being unconsciously insulting and of being vexed if insulted back. On the football meadow he ordered the boys about and even gave orders to men who were twice his age. But since he was going to be a priest he was allowed a certain amount of scope. In addition he gained some respect as being one of the finest kickers of a ball with both feet.

"Leave down that ball," he ordered in an authoritative voice which in the hardness of its timbre and squealy echo reminded listeners of his fathers. He was like his father, too, in appearance, even moreso since his last spell in college. He had become thin and wiry. His little eyes had become narrower, with a touch of the sinister in them.

INTERVAL

The important character in our story is not, however, Peter Devine but Patrick Kavanagh whom we left back there on page 22 as he sat in on an insufferable house party. The reader will be glad to learn that he has not been sitting at the party all this length of time, and that he escaped the company with minor scars.

We now continue the narrative of Patrick's pilgrimage through Dublin during the late nineteen-thirties and early forties—— as we put aside the inevitable progression of the Devine family to Dublin where they occupy a prominent position in the business, social and artistic life of the city. They had no difficulty establishing themselves and being accepted in a city which had at that time so many others of similar background.

Before we meet the Devine (now De Vine) family in this new setting we may perhaps add the following information that the reader might not on his own be able to deduce.

Shortly before the family moved permanently to Dublin Mrs. Devine had become quite odd in herself, as the saying goes, and the family had her committed to the county lunatic asylum. Paddy Devine finally made it to the priesthood. His younger brother Henry married a niece of the Archbishop of Dublin and is in the business world and the world of art. Mary married a young medical doctor, Dr. Cotch, who is now rich and whose public interest is establishing orphanages for Dublin's poor. Jane is as yet unmarried and is a noted pianist.

PART 11

CHAPTER 1

At the end of June two young men were sitting on the side of a cliff overlooking a sea of shimmering Mediterranean blue. All around are signs of bourgeois prosperity—— the cottages of well-off writers, the summer (and sometimes permanent) residences of big city businessmen. A pleasantly beautiful place if at times a little too touristy, too much of just the right blend of the unusual and the commonplace. Trees and flowers and natural rock gardens are trained the slightest bit to be unnatural.

This is Killiney—— a small fashionable area outside of Dublin.

Neither of the two men was thinking deeply on the question of the scenery. The blue sea was observed through the filter of their own problems; the hills around were lovely reflective hills but these two men looked across at them over the hills of their own subjective thoughts.

Anyone looking at these two men would say that here were two happy holiday-makers, freed from the dust of the city, come for the week-end to enjoy the uncomplexed heart of suburban living.

One of the men was slightly older than the other and he also seemed to be the more troubled, the more nervous. He kept turning round to get a better seat but did not remain long in any one position; he shrugged his shoulders like a man who had the itch-- nerves, a habit he had taken with him from the handles of a plough, perhaps, when he had left the country some years before. This habit was more his undoing—— for undone he had been many times—— than many more important things. But he was not aware of this: he imagined that men are judged by their main principles and not by the little things. He scratched his head: he yawned. Sometimes he would sit up straight as if he had sighted something extraordinary passing on the sea-road below.

Except for these peculiar habits he was a normal man, fairly good-looking and far more attractive than his looks would appear to deserve. He was aged over thirty but looked fantastically younger—— the poetic streak, being itself a native of the Land of Perpetual Youth, keeps its possessors young. And keeps them virtuous-looking too even when they may have been less than saints. Perhaps he was truly virtuous. Perhaps what looked out of his eyes was the judgment of the gods. Virtue is often confused with what is narrow of heart, bitter. Patrick was not bitter or narrow-hearted. Nothing seemed to make him bitter or a pessimist.

Though for over six years he had been engaged in the only valid war—— the war to which there is no armistice—— the war of life, and had been seriously wounded, he came up again and again to continue the battle. And where he had been wounded before, he was wounded again—— the same error, the same weakness. Why was that? He was still trying to find out.

For every man the battle of life has a different meaning but for all men the getting of money is a large part of the incidental background. With Patrick the getting of money—— otherwise, a job—— appeared to be practically all that battle. For six years he had tried everything—— everything that in his foolish heart he imagined to be wires, he pulled. He met a new influential acquaintance and he flattered him for a while and the man promised to do the necessary for him. But nothing ever came of it. He was one of those futile labourers whose only permanent job is pulling the devil by the tail. He had no background, no family, no formal education. He was self-educated.

While the callouses of the plough-handles were still tender on his palms he had read through the literatures of Europe. He was not a profound scholar but just the same he knew a great deal more than the average writer. He had written a novel but had made no money out of it. His three published books of verse had brought him a reputation—— but in addition it brought all the jealousy of mean, pub-crawling Dublin where the chief pastime consists in sneering at serious men who stay at home and work.

He was praised by these public-house critics and he liked the praise for a time—— until he discovered that something poisonous lay at the bottom of it all. That little versifier with the narrow eyes who knew all the gossip of the town had praised him to his face and Patrick was shocked and puzzled when he heard that this same person was giving quite a different opinion behind his back. But Patrick kept no spite. Why should he keep up spite? The in-

130

jury is all to oneself when one hates or is bitter. Love your enemies is a sound doctrine for in loving one's enemies a man vanquishes them, while in hating them he vanquishes himself.

Patrick loved simply, though not deeply, because that is what gave him pleasure. Sometimes he deliberately set out to hate people, and though hating by all the rules of warfare seemed the proper thing to do, it was always a failure with him. A friend had put him up to these hates on some occasions and, in despair, seeking the secret of life, he experimented. Little by little he was getting terrified of hating.

He was weak, easily led. He knew that his will was weak but could do nothing about it. From his mother he had inherited this weakness of character. In one way Patrick was thankful to her because, had it not been for this weakness of his mother's will he would probably never have been born. And it was a good thing to be born.

He had a hard struggle but he had also much happiness. He had known the love of beautiful women. This day, the love of a beautiful girl coming into his thoughts, made the scene about him and the sea below him insignificant, not worth a thought. He could love the scenery and the sea too but only as an aside. The light of the intangible Truth had flashed across the hills to him and, that he knew, was something to be grateful for, something worth being born to misery for.

He had seen that light flash on the hills: it might be the sun going down or it might be nothing nameable at all. It was just the hint of the miracle of Creation that makes poets gasp. He had seen it in streams and in ploughed fields and on roads to fairs in country towns, in among the open gaps of the morning where the ashplants of drovers were swinging. Yet in all that beauty there was something that made a man unhappy. There was a price that had to be paid. And the price for such visions was a high price.

Natural life, lived naturally as it is lived in the countryside has in it none of that progress which is the base of happiness. Men and women in rural communities can be compared to a spring that rises out of the rock and spreads and spreads in irregular ever-widening circles. But the general principle is static. Rural life is all background. Life in cities is not a spring but a river, or rather a watermain. It progresses like a novel, artificially. There is no progression in art; there is none in life. And a man coming from a circular static mood to the forward hurry of city life is at a disadvantage. He must learn to pose. Patrick had not learned to pose. He did not want to pose. He wanted to apply natural laws to an unnatural situation. He was conscious of this at times, but being conscious of a fact is not the same thing as knowing how to act on that consciousness.

The happiness he had known in the country was an unconscious yet superb happiness. Since coming to live in the city six years ago he was beginning to wonder if that happiness he had known was any different from the happiness of a cow or of a vegetable in the sunlight. The people with whom he had to deal had awakened early to life. They had escaped the unconscious of the creative soul at an early age—— by education, by worldliness, by being perhaps superficial.

He thought of Henry De Vine whose "cottage" he could see if he opened his eyes, and the thought terrified him. Henry De Vine was younger than he himself was, and yet he was a director of two large companies, married with a wife and three children, and with a look of profound seriousness about him that made Patrick think of him as a great statesman. No innocence in that face, notwithstanding his support for the Church and things religious.

He would have liked to piece together the history of that family but somehow he could get none of the really useful details. They had been up against him ever since he came to the city, trying to break his way into a livelihood. It was the normal battle of life where to know whom to keep down is the same as a victory for one's own side. There are no neutrals in the battle of life.

The De Vines had power. They had intermarried with money and influence and their ramifications were widespread. So widespread that it would be impossible for a man who had other interests to keep track of them all.

Patrick wanted more than anything else in the world the means to get married and to keep a wife. He had found a beautiful and sensitive girl named Margaret O'Carroll and the thought of his inability to marry her drove him to desperation. The De Vines could help him now and he was anxious to get their help. But he had a peculiar way of flattering people by attacking them! he often said whatever came into his head—— or what most people would say was whatever came into his head, though it seldom was really that. He did not realise that a city is a whispering gallery. In nothing more than in the business of getting money was this gossip more venomous, though it was to be found in all activities. Gossip is the publicity agent of society and its motives are never without point.

For one man to succeed in life or in love—— which is the same thing—— another man must fail.

Patrick did not realise the extent of the jealousy raised by his success with Margaret. He did not realise that he was surrounded by hundreds of men who required only a little more heat to be raving lunatics with jealousy. Life is a madhouse and a battle-field combined.

As a poet, too, he had those who hated him because they thought that being a poet was a free gift of Heaven but something for which a high price must be paid. And yet there were all these people who were all optimism with Christian charity towards all. These were the most poisonous. He sensed these things in a vague way, but had not the energy to become involved in such a world. Hating, gossiping, battling left a man no time for living. There was good in the world too, much good, but when it was a question of survival, ethics did not count. Bit by bit he was learning how the wheels go round.

One of the biggest hopes in his life had been the Bishop of Dublin. This man had taken an interest in him because he thought that he would be able to get inside information about the pagan writers from him. He suspected the bishop of being a slippery customer but saw that he had nothing to lose except his self-respect and stood to gain a lot if the deal went through.

He visited the Bishop regularly and kow-towed humbly. For hours he listened to this man trying to impress a poet with his immense learning and piety. Patrick bowed to the profound wisdom of the bishop while he waited for the money that once again was only a temporary expedient "till a job turns up." Patrick saw the fun of it sufficiently to be cynical and when he was out of the shadow of the Bishop's palace he would relieve his feelings by remarks like "Son of a bitch, I wonder will he come across with a job."

No job came at that time or after, but Patrick did not fall out with the Bishop when the Bishop gave him the hint that he would not be at home for a few months. A man should never fall out with a Bishop. Patrick had deliberately chosen to fall out with many of his supposed friends when after a reasonable trial they proved useless to his purpose. But even in this throwing-over of friends there was something of a method, a sacrifice to the gods, as it were. He had been severely tempted to write a scorching letter to the Bishop telling him what he thought, but restrained himself. And now, wasn't he right? Wasn't he right? How easily a man might make enemies of such a distinguished and influential family as the De Vines —— of which the Bishop was a relative.

For the past two hours Patrick had been discussing, in his typical egotistical fashion, the ins and outs of his prospects with Robert Hinny—— a slick writer who knew everybody and was friends with everybody. Patrick had come out to see this man in his home and to seek his advice on these present problems.

Robert Hinny was smooth, cynical and rich. He had a fat wife and three children. Robert Hinny had brought him out to the hills so he could talk in private. He lit a cigar.

He was weary, he said, listening to others talking of their troubles as if no one in the world had problems except them. He had his own miseries: he had made money, plenty of money, he knew everyone that was anybody, and yet there was something superficial about his life and his acquaintances. There was an absence of a deep purpose. He went to symphony concerts, art exhibitions, to theatres, and he knew by name the performers in all these places, but he was out of it all. These arts and interests were a desperate effort on his part to reach a purpose that would last, that was valid.

Patrick would have been surprised had he been able to see into his companion's heart and to learn that Robert Hinny actually envied him his life. But there was not, of course, any means of knowing the other's heart—— except love—— and he was incapable of that Christly other-love which sees into hearts. As it was, the absence of sympathy on Patrick's part awoke in Robert all those bitter repressed emotions. A thin stream of venom was mixed with his companionable talk, venom too subtle to be noticed.

"And you really believe," said he puffing on his cigar as if it were a cigarette, "you really think they are an old aristocratic family, Patrick?"

"Absolutely certain."

Robert smiled. He raised his voice in the tone of one about to deliver himself of an eternal truth:

"I do not think I ever met a man with such a hopeless knowledge of the world—— in some ways. You have a genius, great genius...." He paused.

Patrick wiggled: the word "genius" was a nightmare to him, a nightmare akin to one of those nightmares in which he found himself among a crowded congregation at Mass without his trousers. That cursed word "genius"—— he knew that whenever a man mentioned the word, that man was not a friend.

"Well, do you think I have a chance?" Patrick asked.

"Of the job? If I had the giving of it I'd wire for you. There's no man in the country half as well qualified as you. I'd say you'd get it easy."

Patrick did not like the way the man spoke. He had heard such talk before and every time he had heard it it was a forerunner of failure. There are signs like that in a man's life, little hints which denote the curve of his destiny. He gets used to seeing the same sign, the same tangent to the orbit around which he is whirled. Just like that it was before, just like that. That was the word another man said, that was the identical situation.

This time there was a slight change in the signs around the unbreakable fairy ring of fate. Patrick had achieved these diversions off the old rut by an effort of will. Will can change a man's destiny, the five percent that is changeable, and Patrick had struggled hard to overcome his weaknesses.

And for this job as Publicity Director for the mighty, newly formed Plastics Company, he had pulled every wire, he had gone all out. The girl whom he was hoping to marry had advised him that nothing less than everything a man had got, was any good in the struggle. She had told him everything. She had helped him to look ordinary. His hair was brushed, his nails were clean, his clothes were a modest dark dye. He looked like a responsible bank-clerk, sufficiently miserable and repressed to be entrusted with a well-paid job.

He had got a letter from the Bishop's secretary telling him that his Lordship would do everything in his power to help him if Patrick would call out. Unfortunately, the letter said, his Lordship had little influence in these wordly affairs. But he would do his best.

The letter gave great hope to Patrick. He felt that the Bishop's good offices alone would be sufficient to pull-off the job. But just

135

to make assurance double sure he saw Father Raspoon and that monk gave him his solemn promise to do what **he** could though he doubted that he had much pull in matters of that description. Father Raspoon had stopped writing verse and was now taking a deep interest in art. He had made a tolerable collection of modern paintings at an extraordinary cost. When Patrick called on him he was asked to have a look at the pictures. He praised them to the limit of his capacity for flattery but not flatteringly enough for their owner's fancy. Anyhow, he was going to write to a few people who might have some pull.

After leaving Father Raspoon Patrick visited the Editor of the **Musical Critic** who might, he felt, be able to work some influence with the De Vine household, through Jane De Vine, the pianist.

He had done everything he could, had seen everyone that he thought worth seeing and his tension was now at its height. On the following Tuesday the interview would be held and here he was building up his knowledge of life and society, of the way the wheels go round.

The De Vines had power though none of them admitted it; of that he was certain. They claimed to be interested mainly in art, music and religion, but Patrick in his heart belived that they surely must have some grip somewhere. The façade was art, music, religion. What lay behind it? In theory he surmised these truths, but in practice he argued against them. They were a distinguished old aristocratic family; that was the general opinion and Patrick— being as all men are part of public opinion—— shared the public view to a large extent. Perhaps if he had analysed his thoughts deeply he would find that he was deceiving himself. Pietistic self-deception is a common failing and goes so deep sometimes that it becomes a genuine belief. Thus are bigotries born.

"Will you come back to the house and have some tea?" asked Robert Hinny.

Patrick would have liked to have tea with Robert and his wife not so much because of the tea but because he was learning a good deal of the truth of society as it really was—— by the well-known process of elimination. The truth as it began to reveal itself to him was not pleasant but he liked hearing his heart respond to the ex-citement of reality.

At his own flat in the city a poor tea awaited him but the poverty of the food was compensated for by the knowledge that he was going to meet his own beautiful girl, Margaret, that evening.

136

CHAPTER 2

"My goodness," Margaret exclaimed when she saw him, "I never saw anyone so disreputable. Shoes not polished, trousers not creased—— and look at the way you have your tie! Come over here."

She arranged his tie. She looked at his hair. "Have you not got a comb?"

He brought out a comb and began parting his hair. The girl looked at him disappointed. To begin arranging his hair in public!

"And don't walk with such a long step."

After all her training he was nearly as bad as ever, she said. And he thinking that he had achieved the perfect slickness of touch of the man-about-town. He wanted to tell her how delightful she was, how much he cared for her, but she was not interested in those matters.

"If you cared for me you'd comb your hair and polish your boots."

"I can't please you, Margaret, no matter what I do. Am I not a little improved since I met you?"

"A tiny bit," she admitted.

Margaret was a beautiful girl, tall with brown hair and wistful blue eyes. She was so intelligent and so practical! She never said anything about love. She did things to show it in action. She had one idea in her head and that was to help Patrick get a job so they could get married. A man cannot live on a poetic reputation. No one loved the poetic reputation better than did Margaret—— and the merit that created it—— but she wanted her lover to be in an independent position.

"Well, have you any news?" she asked.

"I met Robert Hinny and he liked these poems of mine very much...."

"I know he does," she interrupted, "but did you meet Peter De Vine that you went out to meet?"

"Wait now and I'll tell you."

"Did you meet him?" she asked determindely.

"No, but...."

"Oh, my goodness, you are terrible. Why didn't you see him as you said you would? You went out to see Robert Hinny because you said that he would give you the proper line on the man. So instead of going to see Mr. De Vine you spent the whole afternoon with Robert Hinny. What good will that man be to you next Tuesday?"

"Peter De Vine has no power either."

"Who told you that?"

"I heard it."

"Well, I'm not saying he has any power but I do know that he's a prominent man in the city and it can never do you harm to be on good terms with men like him. You're always falling out with people for no reason. Why do you tell people what you think of them? How many people tell you what they think of you?"

They had come to a dark corner under trees.

"Give me a little one."

"I'll give you no such thing; you're not worth it."

All the same he kissed her and she did not object.

"You're very good, Margaret."

"I wish you had some sense, Patrick, and you'd get somewhere instead of going about the way you do." She turned back, "I must be getting home now."

"Why are you going home so soon?"

"Tomorrow is Sunday and I have to be up for early Mass. I wish you'd come to Mass some Sunday with me. I don't think you ever pray."

"Indeed I do pray plenty."

"Well, I see few signs of it.

They walked along the canal under the trees. The thrushes were singing. Patrick would have been very happy if only he could be sure of that job—— then they could be married.

"Listen, Margaret," he started and stopped again.

"Try to forget about me," she said.

"But supposing...."

"Suppose nothing."

They parted. The girl ran up the steps to her house and waved once. She did not want to encourage those protracted partings which are so futile and so unbusinesslike and which end about four in the morning.

Margaret was a remarkable girl. Perhaps not so remarkable but rather an example of what the love of a woman can be—— hard, to the point, practical.

In repose her mind was deep and soft. Because of her great sympathy she was not only herself: she was the man she wanted and whom she loved. She lived the moment, filling every crevice with its appropriate work. It is said that women have no capacity for long-distance planning or for abstract thought, both of which propositions are totally wrong. A great woman such as Margaret sees far into the future by simply seeing the moment, and the abstract thought—— which was only abstract because seen as a theory—— she understood better than those who philosophise about it. She saw it as applied life around her.

It is true she had no great feeling for poetry or literature but she did understand poetry when it was personified in a man. She recognised it in Patrick and decided in favour of him though she had dozens of young handsome men following her, asking her to come to dances and parties. These offers she gently turned aside.

From the first moment she was conscious of the un-analysable quality of Patrick's presence. It was something that made a poet or a hater of them. With women, it almost always made a lover of them. The majority of women whom Patrick had met were those literary, artistic women who pretend to have an interest in art and letters and who make it an excuse for stupid affectations, make it an excuse for drinking and acting in an "emancipated" way. Patrick disliked all such women; they were repugnant to him and when he met them on the streets or at literary gatherings he did not know their names. This made him unpopular. It is as important to be the friends of these sort of women as it is to be on good terms with bishops. Women of this kind have an immense influence for good or harm. Scorned, they spread the desolation of hell in the path of the scorner. Indeed that scorn had been one of Patrick's greatest errors since he came to the city.

Margaret had been teaching him how to avoid being unfriendly to women like these. One day he met her for tea in a café. He arrived in a wild state informing her—— thinking she would see how jealous his fidelity was—— that he had cut dead a certain wealthy American woman who tried to speak to him. Margaret cried and said that unless he would try to be nice to everyone she would not speak to him again.

"My goodness! my goodness! why had you to do a thing like that?"

Patrick did not really know why he had to do it.

"Speak nice to everyone," she advised, "no matter whether you like them or not. How can you tell who will be your friend? You cannot afford to make enemies all the time. No one can. It costs nothing to make people happy."

Patrick promised to do his best.

Margaret was twenty-one. She was an orphan. Both her parents were dead and she was living with her aunt in the city while she studied at the university for a science degree. She studied hard. Every examination she took at the University she made part of her love for him. She was looking forward to being in a position to help him. They could be independent and have all the things that money gives, as well as all the other things that only God can give—and that God gives to so few.

She was practical but all her practicality was directed to winning that transcendent beauty which was a nimbus of personality around the head of Patrick.

Patrick wanted to be seen with her on the streets just to show-off to his "enemies"—— as he sometimes pretended to believe some people were. He had no persecution mania but pretended that he had, which was perhaps just as bad. Margaret did not want to be seen with him: she did not want to provoke jealousy. She wanted their love to be a private affair. What did it matter that she did not go out much in public with him so long as they both knew why. No, it was not that she was ashamed to be seen with him, she said; why should she pretend to care for him at all if that were the case. "I'd like to do everything quietly. The quiet way is the best way."

"You are marvellous."

She looked at him. "Oh my goodness! Look at the way that tie is again. You are terrible, horrible, disreputable. No wonder if I were to be ashamed of you. Go on home now and write and write and I'll go home and study."

That was the kind of Margaret O'Carroll.

Wonderful too how soon she became an expert on modern painting. She was a far better critic of Sisley, Monet and Yeats

140

than any of the little critics with wizened faces who gave lectures on art to various societies of old women. She knew more about the poetry of Hopkins, Eliot, Yeats and the other well-known poets than all the women members of the P.E.N. Club or of the other literary societies with which society is burdened. And yet she was only a simple young girl with brown hair, a slim waist and a dreamy look of mystical practicality in her eyes.

She had a sad look about her too, and no wonder, for she had lost her parents within a year. It was that sorrow that made her wise. She had to depend on herself. She had, it is true, some money left by her parents—— but of sympathy, of family affection she was totally bereft.

This circumstance gave Patrick the opportunity to meditate on the problem of sorrow and to try to understand why it is that through sorrow alone a man or woman comes to the true Tree of Knowledge whose fruit when eaten, leaves not behind the bitter remains of banishment, the sting of pleasure.

It was nearly a year now since they had met and the time had passed quickly. Patrick would say to her: "Next week I'll be rich" and she would laugh, and afterwards repeat: "Next week you'll be rich." They had good times together. Not that they were long together. When he wanted to linger she always ran off to study.

She went to Mass every morning. She wanted Patrick to go to Mass oftener though she had no wish to make a voteen out of him. She prayed first and then she studied. Patrick prayed very seldom. His only prayer was a prayer that he might have Margaret for a wife. In a somewhat desultory way he asked that boon of the Blessed Virgin and said three Aves towards that end every night before going to bed. He felt that in the end his prayers would be answered and he promised that he would not become bitter like Goethe no matter what happened.

Looking back on his life from this moment he saw that God had been good to him, that He had kept him on the road to happiness–despite the fact that what he was praying for did not come to fruition. A man does not know what to pray for. A man should only thank God and ask for whatever is really good for him. The lines of George Russell came into his mind:

All our prayers are answered,
O to be wise in prayer!

Margaret prayed for the immediate things which in her woman's way, she knew was the road under her feet which ended at the horizon where all that is beautiful, true and of the poet, rises up to the floor of Heaven. She prayed that she would pass her examination, that she would have good health, that Patrick would learn to be wise and easy-spoken, that he would write every day, that he would learn not to go out in public in a disreputable manner, with his hair tossed and his boots unshined and his tie crooked. Of these, she knew, is the Kingdom of Heaven.

On the following Sunday he saw her at Mass and tried to be home with her at least part of the way. But instead, she went off quickly with a young woman who, as far as Patrick could make out, was a relation of Dr. Cotch and a coming pianist. This girl was also a part-time actress and Patrick didn't much like her. He wondered somewhat why Margaret, who was so good a judge of people should trouble to walk with her and not with him.

That same Sunday he worked hard writing until about five in the evening when he got tired of being alone in his room.

He went down the street on the off-chance of meeting Margaret but though he passed her window several times she made no appearance. So he went down town and into a pub. Even though it was Sunday there were liable to be some literary men there with whom he could talk. He didn't like literary pub-crawlers and normally ignored them unless he were bored. He couldn't even recall most of their names and this was no way of making himself popular.

A newspaper editor was in the pub with a few of his cronies around him. Patrick ordered a drink and sat at the table beside the editor. He liked the editor though he did not respect his opinions. The editor was his friend in a way, but not in the big way that meant something.

They were talking about the De Vines when he joined in the discussion. Gossip. It struck Patrick at the time how interested those men were in gossip. A shallow man listening would say it was idle gossip, but an experienced man would know that no gossip is entirely idle, that in general gossip is the Intelligence Department of business, of jobbery. Months before a job was vacant these men would have guessed about it and would have plans laid.

The editor was a great friend of Patrick as far as praising him in the newspapers went, or of allowing him to say his say in its columns and paying him a small fee. But to take him into the inner ring of his confidence where the gossips plan the commercial future of the state—— this he had not done. Remarkable too how interested really all these pub writers were in literature or in art. Their chief topic was jobs that were going or that were gone and how to circumvent someone's chances in favour of one of the "boys". Patrick only vaguely guessed at this at the time. But a reasonably intelligent man, a man with an average sense of the realities of society as it operates would have a full conscious knowledge of it and would not even consider it sufficiently interesting to comment upon it. To Patrick some of the elemental principles of capitalistic society were sensational discoveries for him—— when eventually he did discover them.

"I didn't see you there last night," said a lantern-jawed fellow with a crooked pipe in his hand as he looked across his glass at Patrick, thinking he had caught the thread of the discussion.

"Where was that?" asked Patrick.

"De Vine's gramophone recital." He turned to the editor and spoke in a different tone, far more intimate, "That was a good thing, that recording of Menuhin."

The editor took a hurried sip of his drink, looked wise, lit his pipe, then answered by asking another question—— directed at Patrick.

"What happened George Flabb that he isn't going back to that radio job?"

"Tired of it, he told me."

The editor drank that in with his whiskey. The other man made a casual remark about golf.

"Where is he living now?" asked the editor.

Patrick explained innocently like a child, for that is what he was in these affairs.

"Have a drink," said the editor, "Joe, Joe," he called the barman.

"What is it?"

"I'll have nothing," said Patrick.

"Fair enough," said the editor.

The man with the lantern-jaws whispered something to the editor and the editor inclined his ear. "Surely," he said.

Then turning to Patrick: "Do you know anything about this job that's going in the Plastics company?"

"What job?" said Patrick, looking a little too surprised.

143

The other man interrupted again and the conversation between the editor and him continued in a whisper—— that is insofar as the main threads were concerned.

Wasn't it odd, thought Patrick, that these big men should be interested in such a small job as that vacant in Plastics? He was somewhat shocked but not unduly so.

The lantern-jawed fellow was a high official in the Civil Service. He was on terms of deep intimacy with all the leaders of the trade – and art—— as far as it was possible. He was one of those numerous members of the public who are forever on the look-out for some harmless "act" of which the ordinary layman and humbug can be a noisy part. Music, the theatre, painting, the people who in general carried on these arts were of the middle and lower upper classes, in recent years of the business classes almost exclusively. Writers were different; they were harder to get on with and to get in with– except for those that drank in pubs and who didn't write. Men like this Civil Servant found much emotional satisfaction in being in the swim of music, art, the stage and such like.

"A wonderful family," the Civil Servant remarked aloud after a short whispered discussion.

"The De Vines?" said Patrick. "I wonder if they are. I shouldn't be surprised if they came from a vulgar background. I know the pianist to see—— and to hear—— unfortunately, and I'd say she hasn't a great deal of breeding."

The Civil Servant became very angry. The editor smiled. Then the former said: "They are the De Vines of Dirnaugh, a well-known family."

"I see," said Patrick dryly.

A young man wearing outlandish clothes at the far side of the pub cocked his ear. The editor gave him a friendly nod. The young man picked up his glass and came across the floor carrying it with him, which to the ironic eyes of Patrick seemed somewhat undignified.

The remainder of the conversation was in the main about literature and art. But beneath all the talk the currents of the De Vine river gave a direction to the most casual remarks. You could sense it. Patrick sensed it, but that was because he was in the market himself with something to sell. These others would have been experts on the trends of such markets even when they had no interest in the business proceeding—— which indeed was very seldom.

144

For a while the discussion turned on the skill of various musicians in the city. Was Jane De Vine the greatest pianist in Europe? She had the poetic touch, it was agreed.

The editor talked about prose. He referred to his Leaders as prose though they were merely a higher type of cliché than was usual in journalism. He asked Patrick what he thought of certain poets and Patrick said they were execrable.

The editor smoked his pipe and took all in without showing any signs of unusual interest.

Closing time! They all went into the street and about their different businesses.

Patrick began to analyse the discussion. Now he was reading into it more than was implied and that was as bad as his usual way of reading less. The wise man takes the crookedness of life and of society as a matter of course and always acts on the principle that the other fellow is trying to double-cross him.

He suspected the editor of being unfriendly which was not quite true. The editor was as near friendly as it is possible for a man to be to another who is neither in a position to return the friendship in tangible form, or a relation, or a member of the same Lodge or Old School Club.

That evening the poet spent in writing love sonnets to Margaret. There was no better way of reaching a woman's affection than by writing poems to her. And who was better equipped to woo in this manner than he? The dilettantes did it and got away with it. Still, he was not fully satisfied with his poetic labour of love, not just because the sonnets were as bad as the usual sincere love poems, but because he had promised the girl to make it his business to write to the Bishop of Dublin that evening to make certain that this great ecclesiastic would do his stuff when the time came. He did not write to the Bishop because in his private mind he had doubts about the Bishop's friendship.

There was a curious something about the Bishop's way of being friendly to him that didn't fit in with Patrick's ideas of a Maecenas. He remembered that the Bishop had once suggested to him to take a menial job in a timber factory at three-ten a week, and on another occasion had worked influence to get him a porter's job in the Civil Service. That was the Bishop's attitude towards the writer. It was the business of the writer to build himself up, to be strong, to dictate to bishops and businessmen. He could do this if only he could strengthen his will, give up all useless habits such as cigarettes, drink—— he was a light drinker—— give up everything, every will-reducing pleasure till he was a giant among pygmies.

He took the packet of cigarettes he had bought and flung it into the fire-grate. Then he covered the flaming packet with ashes and paper to make sure it burned.

He looked through the window at the sun sinking beyond the Dublin mountains and he felt himself a new man, a man upstanding, a man who would go places, a man who would write better than ever. He looked at the sonnets and cast them aside for the present. He would begin a novel—— now that he had begun a new life.

He started on a new page but somehow the words were forced, untrue to experience. This might have been because of his giving up the cigarettes so he went to the fire grate and managed to extract an unburned cigarette, to see what effect it would have. Yes, he could write more freely now. But he got tired and because he was smoking, the passing of time did not seem a waste of time. Two hours passed. He wished he could see Margaret. But she was studying.

All would be well if he got that job. It would give him just that security which would stabilise him. And in a short time the chances were strong that he would be able to give it up and make a good living entirely by his pen. He put his hand in his pocket and took out some silver and copper. He counted it and found that it amounted to three shillings and fourpence halfpenny. But he wasn't too worried. He had a cheque coming from a newspaper on Tuesday and that would carry him along.

In the meantime he had a powerful chance of getting fixed up in a job—— a job at six hundred a year. He was beginning to daydream about how he and his bride would spend the money. They would have a maid and a telephone and they would have nice furniture. Live probably in Fitzwilliam Square, in a flat. But had he gone all out as Margaret had advised? He satisfied himself that he had. He satisfied his conscience that he had done a fair day's work. Anyhow, tomorrow he would tackle that novel in earnest.

He cooked his own tea on the gas cooker on the landing. Having partaken of a good meal of rashers and eggs he felt more like work. But he also felt like another cigarette. He went to the grate, searched in the ashes, and found another not completely destroyed. He shamefully extracted it. Not merely was it his positive belief in the will-destroying nature of pleasure, above all of narcotic pleasure; he had also in his subconscious, superstitious soul a notion that unless he conquered the cigarette habit he would not conquer the world not to mention the city of Dublin. Also to support this superstition—— for superstitions are seldom baseless– his girl Margaret had appealed to him to give up the cigarettes. You will get a job when you go off the cigarettes, that is what his subconscious had always been telling him. He was ashamed. He would go off the cigarettes for Monday and Tuesday and that perhaps would appease the gods. There was far more to the superstitious belief than that, he realised. Oh, he would try to strengthen his will.

CHAPTER 3

Monday was warm. The streets were like an oven. The waves of heat passed over the people as they were going to work, leaving them like vegetables, hardly animate beings. Patrick was strong enough. His mind was edged with resolution. The birds in the trees in the middle of O'Connell Street sang in the hazy atmosphere. The noises of the buses and the traffic was a dim head-choked hum. Patrick was going to visit a few people who had some influence.

First he called on a doctor. The doctor had no influence, he said, not as much power as would drag the scum off boiled milk. Those were his words. But he did know someone who might be able to help. Who? Dr. Cotch. Did Patrick know Dr. Cotch?

"I know his wife's sister."

"That would do alright. Supposing I give you a note for her."

The doctor had the pen to his nose, cogitating whether to use the little influence he had on a stranger or to keep it for some of his own distant relations who might be looking for jobs one of those days. In the end he decided that he would phone instead. The phone was more personal, he said. You could say over the phone what you couldn't say in a letter.

"The pianist, you know?"

"Yes," said Patrick like a schoolboy. "I'm afraid I sort of once gave her a bad write-up in a paper I had been asked to write for. She was giving a concert and I may as well tell you I said what I thought: that I didn't think there was much to her but technique."

"My God!" the doctor said. Then he smiled and appeared to be pleased rather than otherwise; "Oh, she won't keep that in for you."

"Do you think I have much of a chance?"

"I think you have not only a chance: I think you'll get it easily."

In a rather shaky condition of hopefulness Patrick called on Dr. Cotch's wife having first phoned Jane De Vine's secretary to know if he might use the pianist's name. The secretary informed him that the pianist was engaged but that she supposed it would be quite alright.

The unconventional approach is always extremely dangerous when dealing with suspected parvenus who are terrible sticklers for the formula. But in Patrick's case there was not much chance of the conventional approach. Time was short. Convention is usually the longest way round which is to say the shortest way home.

With all the trepidation of Villiers de L'Isle Adam lingering on the doorstep of his publisher's house, Patrick went up to Dr. Cotch's door. He waited a moment to gather courage. He took off his hat and holding it in his hand more or less against his belly he decided that this was altogether too abject a gesture. He wished he had come without a hat. He waited a moment. A car pulled up at another house and a doctor got out. Very confident, that doctor was, full of himself, though in Patrick's judgment he was an indifferent sort of being, a poor thinker. But he had the confidence that Patrick lacked, that poets in general lack, and that Dublin and Ireland try to destroy in every creative thinker.

Standing at the doorway Patrick began to feel that he was being observed. He was fairly well known. Doctor's and professional men's wives are every bit as inquisitive—— if not more so—— as the humblest peasant woman leaning across a gate in Galway or Leitrim. Taking his courage in at least one hand—— or one finger— he pressed the doorbell and turned away, waiting. In a momentary glance he saw the Square with its trees and its shrubs and at that moment the intimate Square was peeping through the iron railings staring at him. A most uncomfortable feeling.

A maid opened the door. She gave a frightened start on seeing the man notwithstanding Patrick's attempted conventional stance and nonchalance. That was not a good augury.

Who did he want to see? Mrs. Cotch. What name was she to give?

"Patrick Kavanagh."

"Have you an appointment?"

"You can say I'm a friend of Miss Jane De Vine."

"Well, wait there, will you?"

The maid went off in her still frightened mood. Patrick looked around him idly at the pictures in the hall. He couldn't imagine

149

any person with an artistic sense permitting such gross vulgarity to desecrate the hall of their house. Pictures of flowers that seemed to have been painted by machinery, a statue in a corner that was clearly made in the same automatic way. Here was a picture of Highland cattle standing ankle deep in the stream. They had tremendously long horns. Patrick was unable to keep still; so anxious was he, that he kept walking up and down the hall. He ran his hand along the brass railing that ran from near the door for about ten feet, a railing which was a tribute to the drunken eighteenth century when the owners of these houses coming home late at night sidled sideways towards the light by the aid of this directing rail.

Presently the lady of the house came out. She stared rudely enough at him.

"Who are you?" she asked.

"Kavanagh, I'm a writer."

"What paper do you write for?"

This remark showed Patrick that kind of person viewed writing in terms of newspapers. Or rather it should have shown him. As it happened, it merely made him ill at ease, left him searching for excuses.

"I know your sister."

"Ow, I see."

The woman who was fat and looked as if she were made without any bones worth speaking of, spoke in an affected voice—— an Anglo-Irish accent that had no warrant from any country or place in any part of the world. An invention merely to show the ordinary folk that they were a different breed. So highly inflected, so gross and so unnatural was it—— when it was a vogue, which it no longer was—— that no self-respecting peasant would use it. So these miserable aristocrats who had enough money to act like ordinary folk and too much to be honest, had the exclusive use of the most appalling accent that was ever known.

"I was looking for a job with the Plastics Company and I came wondering if you would put in a word for me with Peter De Vine who I am told is your father."

"Mr. Peter De Vine," she emphasised the "Mr." and she appeared to Patrick's way of thinking to have that high degree of insultability which he had noted among women of lowly birth who were keeping a precarious hold on social heights to which they had un-

150

worthily climbed.

"Dr. Bloit phoned you, I think," said Patrick.

Obviously Dr. Bloit had not used up that quantity of his influence that a phone-call would require.

The woman led him to the waiting room and standing before him put a number of questions.

What books did he write? Were they really published? and so forth. She was well acquainted with the world of painting, stage and executant music but she was weak on poetry and literature. Only in sofar as the Saturday literary page of *The Irish Times* gave poems publicity, she knew nothing—— except what she had learned at school, perhaps.

Patrick found it embarrassing to be his own publicity agent. He hesitated before mentioning some of his works and the result was that she partly disbelieved his story. Eventually he began to take pleasure in the woman's ignorance of him, was delighted in a bitter sort of way and, instead of saying something nasty, as he normally would, he bore with her and observed her closely. She was about thirty-eight years old; she had small clubby feet and walked with a short step. She was the sort of woman whom Patrick had found among the fiery, patriotic sections, those who were always looking for something or someone to hate with a good conscience. When Patrick realised this he was uncomfortable. His slightest remark might be construed as an attack on some cherished institution or idea. He would not be surprised to discover that she was a strong supporter of the Gaelic language revival but knew not a word of the language herself.

Now that he remembered, she held At Homes every Tuesday evening to which all the most attractive illiterates—— in Patrick's view—— were invited. All the repressed would be there, ex-poets, actors, journalists, patriots.

While Patrick was considering all these things the woman was talking about race-horses. Patrick was well acquainted with race-horses through reading the newspapers and he lived up to Mrs. Cotch's opinion of herself. It was however a strain and he was glad when she drew his attention to the pictures.

There were two Osbornes which Patrick was about to speak of when the woman pointed out another picture, a reproduction of some machine-made painting—— and she screwed her shoulders before this in the manner of excruciatingly artistic people.

151

"Isn't that good?"

"I prefer one of these."

"Those are terrible."

Patrick could see at once that the woman was now having an artistic mind of her own—— a most fashionable idea even when wrong. The real truth was that she, and the others who created fashion in this manner, was dressing up vulgarity to make it look as near as possible to an artistic virtue. She knew what she liked— and she liked loud-coloured pictures, dresses and furniture, and she was only biding her time till the fashion permitted an open attack on the tedious things of the aesthetic spirit.

It might have been that Patrick was misjudging the woman; he was inclined to jump to conclusions sometimes, to act on impulse. But when he saw her spit in the fire he was more than ever confirmed in his opinion. There was surely something in Robert Hinny's suggestion that the De Vines were not all they claimed to be. But Patrick knew that he would have to deceive himself for only a few days more and then, if things did not work out right, these people would know what he really thought of them and their pretensions to art.

Why had he stooped to these people at all? Perhaps the De Vines had no power worth speaking of. Only a façade. Then the signs of wealth that he saw around him cast a halo that befogged his judgment: the big house with all its rich, loud furniture, the grand piano that he saw in the next room as he came in and which someone was now playing; the divans, the chairs, the whole assembly of prosperity was the apotheosis of the normal which became remote and worshipful as he contemplated it all.

He was so weak, or, so seemingly weak. That was another of his defects. He gave the impression of weakness, of being a common inarticulate clod and it is the impression that counts. Successful living is like a work of art, it is the illusion we give that is effective. A man may be a great poet or a great philosopher but if he fails to give that impression to the world he will have a hard time of it—— though ultimately he will be no less great. And thus many true poets had to wear the insignia of their trade—— the black bow-tie, the broad-brimmed hat, the dreamy eyes. It pays.

On the other hand Margaret had advised him to play the role of the ordinary clerky fellow. She had, it is true, also suggested his trying it the other way, but to carry off successfully the grand pose, as Yeats did, requires an essential greatness that is superior to the pose. And did not Yeats pay the price for his pose in the artificiality of his work, in its coldness?

"That's my daughter, Kate, playing," Mrs. Cotch said when she noticed that Patrick was listening—— or appeared to be. Actually, he was trying not to hear, for the sounds coming from the piano were not very musical.

"Is she going to take it up professionally, Mrs. Cotch?"

"Ow, now, She is going on the stage."

"My goodness," Patrick added.

"I had intended going on the stage myself, but father needed me to look after the stables and I had to abandon the idea."

"Too bad."

"Yes, and I had a real talent for it, too. Are you interested in the stage?"

"Not in the actors; I'm interested in dramatic literature, naturally. But the plays I see performed here are generally poor."

"But don't you think MacLiammoir is splendid? I told him the last time he was here that he should go in more for the better class humorous play like those by Noel Coward. Did you see Muriel in **The Bride?**"

Mrs. Cotch went on and on about actors. It was plain that she had no other interest in the theatre save the shoddy emotion of knowing the players. Her daughter, coming into the room, ostensibly to look for something, sheets of music maybe, cut off the woman's disquisition on actors much to Patrick's delight. The daughter—— to whom Patrick would like to have been introduced but was not—— was a pretty girl of about seventeen. Patrick had often seen her parading on Grafton Street and he used to wonder who she might be. He once or twice had a mind to speak to her in cafés where they sat at the same table but there was just that touch of the dance-hall flirt about the girl which made him shy of an unorthodox approach. Girls of that description have a talent for making wise men and noble-spirited poets feel mean and humble. Bad as the hangers-on to the tail of the arts were and bad as the pub-critics of both sexes were they were an improvement on such as this girl seemed to be.

Considering her mother's figure and face, the girl was extraordinarily well-made. Good food, good housing can do that with indifferent material. She gave Patrick a sly look as she whisked out of the room.

It was about time he got down to the business for which he had come. He had still several other people to see before night. He put the question: "Could she do anything about the job?"

Once again it was Patrick's fate to be unnecessarily surprised: the woman knew all about the job. Was there anyone but himself who didn't know about every job, however small, that was going?

Mrs. Cotch thought that any sort of pulling would have no effect—— the job would go by merit alone. Anyhow, her family were only simple artistic folk—— that is what she sought to convey—— who did not delve in such mundane matters.

"And what about His Lordship, the Bishop?"

His Lordship wouldn't dream of having anything to do with such a business. He was too busy on committees, organizing aid for the poor and the other thousand and one jobs that a bishop who *is* a bishop has to engage in. But it could do no harm to try seeing that Patrick already had an acquaintance with him.

Leaving the woman, he did not feel that he had furthered his cause very much. It might well be, he reflected, that it would have paid him better to have stayed at home writing verse. Does God give a man a gift that he may starve by it? Did not Christ mean that a man should do the work he was born to do, finding through it his salvation—— when he advised to seek first the Kingdom of God and His justice? But could men be mere cold automatons? Did not a poet desire to have a wife as the rich man desires to have several?

He went into a restaurant and had a cup of coffee. Counting his cash after paying for the coffee he found that he had less than two shillings. How was he going to get money now? He went to the newspaper office and after much humiliation he got paid two pounds in advance.

Now with two pounds in his pocket he became a changed man, an optimist. He saw goodness everywhere around him. The sunny streets and the crowds and the buses were all smiles. He felt that he was progressing. He was in great luck this day. He returned to the restaurant and had a second cup of coffee. At his table three men were discussing trade, the price of sewing needles, no less. A large consignment was coming in shortly and, from what hints he could gather, the De Vines were interested in sewing needles. After a short while one of the men commented casually on the job that was going in Plastics and one of them said: "George will make it, I suppose."

"Yes, the brother is interested in Jane. Did you hear her last Sunday?"

"No, I was out golfing at Hermitage. J.J. was there."

"Were you talking to him?"

"A minute."

The men then changed the subject to the play that was running at the Gaiety and Patrick was no longer interested.

In what indecipherable hints did these men and women of the world convey their meaning to one another. The outsider remained outside. It was obvious by now to Patrick that beneath and beyond his own world of theory lay another more sinister world, the world of jobbery where no poetic or Christian ethics ruled. Sinister. Sinister.

Wandering along the quays while waiting for the bus that would bring him to the Bishop's palace he looked upon the loafers, the unemployed, and could feel a new sympathy for them. They had not for one single moment awakened and become aware of life.

The tragedy is to be aware of the true state of affairs and yet be unable to do anything about it. Not so much to be aware of things as they were but to realise somewhat darkly that another world, another society, was underwriter to the world of the spirit and the mind. Patrick was doing his best to break in and those who were within were doing all in their power to keep him out.

CHAPTER 4

However, there was the Bishop. No matter what anyone might say Patrick still believed the De Vines had power to help him and that they were inclined to be willing to help him if he gave them the chance—— the excuse.

The Bishop was walking in his garden in the company of a man whom Patrick recognized as one of the leading manufacturers of the city. He remembered him well. He was a prominent member of the Society of St. Vincent De Paul, a member of the Boards of several large city hospitals, a pious man.

It was this man, that some years before, had offered Patrick a menial job after being recommended by the Bishop. Patrick had been advised on no account ever to refuse anything that looked like an opening; he called on the man and went through his factory. He employed several hundred slum girls. Patrick walking through the unhygienic workshops where the dust and grime of the city clung black and germ-laden to the tools and floors, took pity on the girls and wondered how that good and holy man who owned the factory could so shut his eyes to this form of prostitution—— for that is what it ultimately amounted to.

The Bishop knew of it all. He must have known that girls working in such conditions for a pittance could not help thinking that they would be far better off on the streets. Some of these girls went out drinking with the young sons of the nouveau riche and some of them—— Patrick knew—— lived in Merrion Square as the mistresses of these young men. Should these things be mentioned? Doubtful. The big businessman, who was big in body as well as in purse—— thick-set, large jowls, savage determination in his eyes—— he and the Bishop were as thick as thieves. The Bishop was wearing his purple skull cap to shield his bald head from the burning sun. Now and then they would stop and turn towards each other in deep intimate conversation. Patrick could see them through the green shrubs as he came up the drive. He was considering whether to allow himself to be seen now and await developments or ring the bell and see the Bishop's secretary. He rang the bell. As he did so the Bishop and his thick-set companion were preparing to part company. Patrick guessed that the Bishop had either seen him or sensed him.

He met the secretary, a simple, humble young priest who, of course, could see no difference between a poet and a beggar. The tracks of beggars are many around the back doors of Bishops' palaces, and the secretary and staff develop an instinct for dealing with beggars alone. This is not the best sort of moral development, is not quite in keeping with Christ's teaching—— or is it?—— but it is the way it happened.

In an ideal society a poet coming to a Bishop's house would be treated as an honoured visitor, but—— times and fashions have changed.

Patrick knew he should have stood on his own two feet, that he should have stayed at home and worked—— till, as Emerson says, the Bishop or whoever else was necessary to him would come to visit the poet.

Degradation, degradation, degradation, he cried to himself as he sat in the waiting-room listening to the little smooth-faced priest who was so innocent and so empty of all the great crude vital qualities which are wild but benevolent tyrants that guard the tabernacle where the Muse reposes.

"Lovely day," the priest remarked gently and offered the poet a cigarette.

The poet was not smoking till after the interview.

"His Lordship should be here any moment now. You go to the Sacraments regularly?"

"Not as often as I should," Patrick replied like a child.

Oh, how mean, how undignified he felt! Was this the patronage the Church offered to the literary man? Perhaps this was the patronage, did we know the facts, that was offered to Michaelangelo. Perhaps he too stood humbly hat in hand supplicating his great patron. We know he was humbled. We know how he was made to feel his insignificance and how he thought his work of little merit, unworthy. It is not, and was not, that those in power desired consciously to degrade the artist; it is that by his nature and the nature of his avocation the poet and artist are pliable, childlike, ever remaining too impressionable, too soft of edge.

157

They could conquer the world if they allowed the soft wax of the sensitive soul to become hard as successful men of the world do—— or as successful men of the world seldom have need to do, they being born old and calloused of soul.

At any rate, Patrick's reason explained to his conscience, what you are doing is not compromise, not demeaning; what you are doing, you are doing so you may not be compelled to compromise that which is dearest to you. It is your duty to use this Bishop or anyone else so that you may go on writing. All is well provided that you do not compromise on the main issue.

Throw away one of Atlanta's golden apples, throw away the second, throw away the third, you throw them all away that you may win the race of the gods.

There were no mirrors in the waiting room. The young priest had gone out to see the Bishop and Patrick kept walking around the circular mahogany table looking at the brown wainscotted walls without pictures or decoration of any sort. He fiddled with the blinds, he stared out the window at the hills beyond. It was a rich landscape that spread before him, but he saw no beauty in it. His conscience was still troubled in spite of the efforts of his reason to explain away his cowardily humility. He felt, let his reason say what it would, that his deep poetic soul was being injured somewhat.

Ten minutes passed. The minutes seemed like hours. The round mahogany table was a very vulgar-looking piece of furniture, seemed not part of the furniture of a bishop's palace, more like a piece that had seen service in the lounge of a country hotel; it reminded him of the pictures he saw in Mrs. Cotch's—— the table would make a good centre-piece for a room decorated by such pictures. It set the metronome.

At this moment the Bishop swept into the room like a hostess in evening dress. To look at, but without undue emphasis on the man's character, his entry had the speed, the determination of a hangman calling to the condemned prisoner's cell at five mintues to eight in the morning. He had his head down, he was smiling at the floor. He had a habit of looking at a visitor's boots first. Patrick remembered how when he first met the man he was wearing a pair of broken shoes and the Bishop, looking as it seemed at the shoes, embarrassed him. The fact is that the Bishop hardly saw the shoes at all. It was a habit of his born out of some far hidden spiritual defeat of his ancestors.

The Bishop of Dublin was not the typical bishop at all. He was spare of flesh and slight of build, about five feet seven or eight in height. His face was hard and his mouth tight. There were three large furrows in his brow; his head was bald. A man looking at him with the objectivity of one who had nothing to lose or gain by knowing the man would say that here was a man of deep cunning. Not a pernicious cunning perhaps but a sharp knowledge of the world. His grey long face was the face of an ascetic, or of a dealing man from some mountainy district in the county Leitrim.

Patrick had too much to lose if he lost the Bishop to be able to see the man in an objective way. None the less he was not deceived, for out of the Bishop's presence, in the days when he had first known him he could discard the man quickly and effectively. "Son of a bitch". He should have more respect for a bishop of the church. As a bishop he had respect but he was not a respecter of persons, except as a pretence, when as now he wanted to get something out of a man. But his pretence was of no avail. The Bishop saw through the mask. It is useless pretending to be something one is not in some degree fundamentally at heart. The Bishop was no fool though he was not the kind of wise man he ambitioned. He had a conceit as a scholar, as a writer, but his Lenten Pastorals were poor enough. Patrick read them carefully and on one occasion ventured to suggest improvements without effect.

"Well, my good man," the Bishop said quietly, kindly. Patrick knelt down and kissed the episcopal ring because there was no one looking. He did not consider that kissing the episcopal ring was something to be ashamed of, but for some reason literary circles in the city were inclined to think that being slightly anti-clerical was the natural corollary of the artistic vocation. Patrick did not share this notion. He, however, tried to appear as impious as the fashion decreed and prayed in private.

Patrick smiled at the Bishop who had asked him to sit down. "Your Lordship is looking very well" said Patrick.

The Bishop fondled his ring. He glanced out the window.

"Who wouldn't look well in such blessed weather? Aren't those light brown clouds over there in the west very beautiful?

We often look upon the clouds
With tints so gay and bold
But seldom think upon the God

Who tinged those clouds with gold.

God is very good to give us this beautiful country to live in and this wonderful weather. Do you pray much, my child?"

The Bishop was being wonderfully kind, loving; his words belied the harshness of his face and the hardness of his lips. The Holy Spirit had descended on him and had sown on the arid ridges of his thought the poetry of charity. Patrick was moved.

He would have been completely moved, completely won over by the Bishop's talk, had he not this problem on his mind. He had to reserve a part of his mind free from enthusiasm so that he might criticise.

"I was at Mass three mornings last week" said Patrick. He went out to explain how he had years before made the Nine Fridays and the Bishop smiled still more. He was posing now, posing as the religious man who was trying to conceal the fact that he was religious.

The Bishop listened. Patrick, losing some of his critical control ran on. He even forgot what he had promised not to forget in dealing with the Bishop, that this was the man who had offered him a menial job. If he could keep that memory alive he would have the Bishop's proper level of patronage for the arts. He couldn't remember anything so ordinary. Something good would come out of this and all would be forgotten and forgiven.

"Do you think I have a chance of this job, my Lord?"

"Pray, pray. Whatever Our Blessed Lady thinks is for your good you will get. You have a deep devotion to Our Blessed Lady you told me?"

"I have, always had."

"She will look after you". His voice was soft and sonorous and his eyes turned up had a look of love in them. "What I will do is, I will write a note to a friend of mine who may be able to do something for you in the matter."

He took paper from the rack on the table. Patrick offered him a pen but he had his own in the folds of his voluminous garments.

"Have a cigarette."

The Bishop was writing. Patrick took a cigarette but did not light it. What to do during such a time as this when someone is writing a letter for one is a problem as great as confronts a writer when he sits waiting till an editor reads over his manuscript. Sit still. Patrick could not sit still. He picked his ear, his nose, he rubbed his palm across his head. He was sweating; he took out a handkerchief, a dirty one, and wiped his brow.

"There" said the Bishop handing him a sealed envelope, "post that letter when you go into town and call again on Wednesday to tell me how you got on. How are you off for money?"

"I have...plenty."

"Are you sure?"

Patrick was trying to give the impression of high decency, a man poor but too proud to admit it.

"Take these few pounds" said the Bishop.

Disregarding every warning and advice of both Margaret and his own theorizing mind he put out his hand and took those three pounds which in taking he was taking the price of his soul as valued by a man whose trade was souls. As soon as he had the money in his hand he knew that he had made a mistake. Then he made offers to return it which only made matters worse. He lingered and complained till in the end he had sold himself and had by making little of the price antagonized the buyer. Oh, who can teach men the way to accept money? With boldness is the only way.

The Bishop sat with his arms folded. Patrick was standing half way between the table and the door. His Lordship rose.

"My dear fellow," he said, "you go home now and pray as I told you and everything will come well in the end.

Patrick was outside the door. He made a last minute appeal with his eyes to the Bishop standing at the top of the steps, an appeal to him to do what he could. For Patrick felt, not without reason that the Bishop was an expert in the art of letting men down without their knowing it.

Could it be possible that this demeaned man, half running, half walking down the pebbly drive from the Bishop's Palace was a true poet, a man of courage and intellect, a man who was afraid of no man and only sought truth?

But all men as well as poets are like that when they walk with their hearts bare, exhibiting to the world their palpitating moods, their weaknesses.

He posted the letter; he had a mind to open it and see what the Bishop had said. He did not know the name of the man to whom it was addressed.

161

CHAPTER 5

It was coming on evening now. He called into the pub where the poets who did not write met on Monday and Thursday evenings. There they were all of them sitting praising each other and talking literature all the time. "That line had what Belloc called the unwanted spondee," he heard one small particularly stupid versifier say. Although he had written much verse in his time Patrick did not rightly know what a spondee was. The last time he had seen the word was in a text book for the Intermediate examination.

Those men who sought emotional satisfaction by being in the company of writers and artists were there in strength this evening. As soon as a new "writer" came in the door one of these men who liked the company of writers gave him the wink and arranged a place at their table for him.

A fellow with a corrugated face and wearing a large black hat over an expression of profound poetic pessimism entered and was immediately seized by three fat fellows who were dying to taste the company of a son of Apollo.

The editor of the *Irish Times* sat alone, as if in a huff. He was the mountain that forced all the literary Mahomets to come to him; he did not go to them. Now he was waiting there testing his drawing powers. Finally the poet with the corrugated face went over to the editor and leaning on his shoulder made a few solemn humbug remarks.

How seriously these men took themselves!

"Are you coming in or going out?" a little fellow with a long straight pipe in his mouth said to Patrick who was still in the doorway looking on. "Don't be so bloody difficult," he said through his teeth. "Will you have a drink? Joe, Joe.... Of all the men I have met you're the most impossible...."

"No, I'll have nothing, I'll have nothing; I only came in to see a fellow that's not here. I'll be going away in a minute."

"Have a drink," he said with a hard ironic bite.

"I will not."

"Impossible man!"

The conversation at the tables was the usual drivel. There were no standards of criticism. That destructive element of inarticulate Dublin society which became articulate in Gogarty and Joyce was here represented. A poisonous element, bitter, clever, good at making hurtful witticisms about their neighbours. But they had nothing creative to their name. Some of them achieved a reputation— for scintillating wit but the final effect was injury to the soul. They had their innings but that innings was over. Serious-minded men of talent and some of genius came in from the country with fertile imaginations.

Patrick should have felt sympathy instead of dislike for these witty jackeens who could imitate but could not create. He was brutally cruel to their efforts. Why did he not understand that these men would be creative if they could?

They could get jobs; that was the trouble, that was their compromise. They could beat him for all the good jobs. They may have said to themselves: we may not have the joy of writing as well as he does but we will see to it that that is the only pleasure he will have.

Patrick came to the pub because that was the only way he had of hearing about jobs. It was here from the little fellow with the long pipe that he had first heard of the present job.

These poetasters managed wonderfully to be on good terms with everybody that counted.

The fellow who had asked him to have a drink was a great friend of Jane De Vine and had praised her once in the newspaper. The man with the corrugated face was one of Father Raspoon's most intimate friends. There was another fellow who knew the youngest of the De Vines— Hector who kept the racing stable.

All the men in that pub were well-in. Patrick himself knew all the most influential people, but not in the right jobbery way as these men did.

More people came in. The hum of the conversation rose higher. Patrick gave another glance around the room and then decided: "Nobody there," he said to himself in a loud voice.

A few solemn-funny faces looked up.

He went to a restaurant and had a good meal. Leaving the

restaurant he met Margaret.

"Well, any news?" she asked.

"I'll tell you in about two hours more."

She was very beautiful, so modest looking and so noble-looking in her simple blue dress. Her long brown hair—— it was not blonde—— hung down her back. Margaret knew how to wear clothes. Everything she wore was perfectly chosen, always in the fashion. She saw that Patrick was looking at her and she wasn't a bit pleased. That sort of silly carry-on for a man who had no job.

"Who did you see today?"

He told her.

"And are you going out to see the other one now?"

"I am."

"Well, go on and don't be late. Did you phone to make an appointment?"

He hadn't.

"Oh, my goodness me," she sighed, "go now and phone and I'll go home to study."

"When will I see you again?" he called after her.

She screwed her body into a motion of despair. No she would not answer him till he was worthy of an answer. With that she went off leaving Patrick to gape after her lithe, swaying form going in the direction of St. Stephen's Green.

CHAPTER 6

As Patrick saw it, the De Vines had the reputation in the city, and country too, of being people of tremendous goodwill who had very little wealth, having spent it all on good works: builders of churches, supporters of the Foreign Missions, patrons of the arts. They had no money of their own, perhaps, but such was the respect in which their ancient family was held that anything they wanted in the shape of money they could get.

Henry De Vine's wife answered the phone and he was invited to come out. Over the phone her voice seemed to be educated and she herself to be a woman with a genuine interest in poetry. Patrick was full of enthusiasm as he went out by bus. Going up to the doors of the great was almost second nature to him now. There is a trade going up to such doors. One needs to be able to judge the antecedents of the householders. The old aristocracy can be approached in an unorthodox way; the new have thin skins. Patrick smoked the Bishop's cigarette as he went up the path to the hall door. This gave him confidence.

The maid who answered the door was not quite as fearful of visitors as the maid in Dr. Cotch's. Servants are like their masters and a man visiting a house for the first time would do well to study the manners and moods of the maids. This maid was brazen and familiar. It wasn't that she asked Patrick personal questions about his writing and his family, it was that she already knew. She told him. This kind of familiarity had been the bane of Patrick's life for many years and only now was he developing a counter to it—— a haughty imperious pose, completely ridiculous to himself but which had its effect on the other.

"My hat," he said, and handed her that article with careful fingertips as though he were afraid of making contact with her unclean person. She took the hat nervously and called him Sir instead of, as when he entered, Pat.

The lady of the house, Mrs. De Vine, appeared in the hall now and very warmly and sympathetically brought him to the drawing room. She was a gentle woman, handsome, obviously educated, but much afraid of life. She was like a wife who had been beaten. Henry De Vine was out but would be back shortly.

"So you're looking for a job in Plastics!"

She felt that it was a pity a man of genius as he was should have to tie himself down to the slavery of a job.

"A mere wage slave."

"Madam," he said, "the worst of all slaves is a slave who has no wages. I hear a good deal of sentimental talk about the tyranny of money, the drudgery of having to occupy a desk. The drudgery of having none to occupy is a thousand times worse. Some of the greatest poets have been men of business and their art did not suffer. The idea that the poet is a sort of glorious fool who has none of the natural appetites and desires is part of the wicked romanticism of our present day society."

"Money is not everything, my dear," she said.

Looking around the room Patrick saw that it was decorated in excellent taste: the pictures were good and there were hundreds of books. "I used to read a lot," the woman said, "but now with the social life, and...."

Before she could finish the sentence a mumbling, groping was heard in the hall; somebody had come down the stairs. Into the room this somebody presently came. He was an old man, Peter De Vine himself.

In one single body Patrick thought that he had never seen before so much ugliness, His eyelids drooped and his little eyes stripped down to the bottom of the eyeballs implied some horrible disease. Age can be ugly sometimes but not as ugly as this. His nose ran water and every now and then he would rub the watery drop away with his knotty finger.

His voice when he spoke was thin and frightening,

"Who's this boyo?" he inquired in a hard procrustean tone that made the white cat on the rug jump up and run out of the room. The woman raised her voice:

"He's a poet, a writer."

"I knew a damn good poet once in the country," he said as he groped to a deep armchair, "a damn good poet be the name of—— be the name of—— what's this now his name was, Molly?"

"You can remember if you try."

166

"We called him the Bard of Callenberg."

The maid brought in a glass of milk with egg and whiskey in it for the old man. She held the concoction to his lips and he spluttered like a baby.

So this was the father of the De Vine family, Patrick reflected. He did not look like a man of much breeding: there was something of the cattle stable and the pig-sty about his movements and his talk, Patrick admitted in his own mind that he could be mistaken in this. He was wrong before and might be wrong now.

"Me pipe," the old man called sharply.

"The woman rushed to find the pipe. After that the old man spoke no more: he sat puffing at his pipe and occasionally putting his finger to his nose to wipe away the jewel-like drops. He spat in the fire. He scratched himself behind.

The woman of the house felt uncomfortable and tried to open up a discussion on books. The giggling maid kept coming in and going out and the discussion on literature failed to get anywhere. It was odd. The old man's presence had a killing effect on any intellectual conversation that might be started. It was not anything he said—— for he said nothing, just an odd grunt—— but it was his presence.

Patrick, who was forever relating things back to his childhood, remembered such another man in his native parish. When he was sighted coming in the distance by the boys playing at the crossroads the cheers and the laughter and all the fun would suddenly become choked in their hearts and on their lips.

Mrs. De Vine was young and she, without knowing it, was being unfaithful to her husband now. The marriage bond may sanctify by the effect of sacramental grace but something that may be called love or whatever it may be—— for it is intangible—— climbs over the midnight wall of marriage and parts what God—— O not what God—— what money, what economic and social opportunity have bound together. Christian marriage, most ideal of God's gifts when, like God's other gifts, it grows from the natural roots of the Older Law, has an awkard battle to fight these days.

Mrs. De Vine looked at the poet and he looked out the window— chiefly to keep an eye on the soon home-coming Henry, the husband. It must not be thought for a moment that he leaned to the woman's affections, being thus unfaithful to Margaret. He merely allowed whatever of the breath of affection there blew to escape naturally, adding to the communal passion of the world.

"All these books are mine," she said in a meek voice. My husband is only interested in music and in art."

She said this as though she did not believe it and wished to give information with contrary words.

"We have musical evenings here and I really do not love the type of music they play. Quartets and Quintets by Mozart, Bach and Beethoven. Miss Jane De Vine played a piano concerto the last evening and—— O it was very fine. My husband spends a good deal of money on pictures."

"Does he intend to sell them again."

"One never knows, Patrick." She called him by his Christian name and he trembled. Was he being unfaithful to Margaret now? He decided to cut off the stream of the woman's affection by a sudden remark:

"I'm not interested in books, or paintings or in music."

So he had done it again, done what some of his friends had always charged him with doing—— firing on the ships that were coming to rescue him, firing on his friends. It was an impulse and he could not control it. The impulse came up from some depths of conscience, part of his character directing the curve of his destiny.

The woman's attitude changed. She no longer liked him though she said nothing to show it. He felt it in the room like a cold draught. He had experienced this before and now he did not like the experience. He had made a mistake. He should have let the woman spend her emotion on him. But what could he do? He was made that way.

He could now see the course the conversation was about to take when she was rudely interrupted. All he could do was daydream what might have been a happy reality. She was about to tell him all about her husband and her husband's relations, all about her brother Father Raspoon, all about her regrets. He would have learned the secrets which were hinted-at in pubs, the secrets of jobbery and money. Through women the inner life of society is known. Why could he not let women of influence be his friends? There was no infidelity to the One Woman in that.

Henry De Vine came in with a friend, a small fat man who was an art critic—— an assumed art critic. This fellow was also a music lover and was to be seen at all symphony concerts during the winter.

Henry was a small man with a smooth face and a very ingratiating manner; he was one of those fellows who looked too sweet to be wholesome. He rushed to shake hands with the poet. He held Patrick's hand for a long time while he pawed his shoulder with the other hand and asked him if he had seen his collection of French paintings.

"Oh, we must show you them."

Patrick accompanied by the art critic and the owner was led around the rooms where the pictures were hung. Had he been alone he might have enjoyed the pictures but with this man at his side demanding all the time new angles of praise on the works and new suggestions as to their present value in sterling, the excursion was boring. The owner pawed him all over.

"I bought that one for ten pounds."

"Very cheap."

"Starving artist," Henry said without thinking what his words implied. "That's one there for ten. I'd get five hundred for it today."

"Easy," said Patrick.

"See his sense of form," said the critic. "See how he has organised his masses and his blues. Pigmentation is very fine."

The owner was delighted with the art critic. They went into another room where lots of pictures were piled against the wall. Henry took them out one by one for exhibit.

Having seen all the pictures they went into the gramophone and music library. There were two grand pianos here.

"Put on the Ninth," said the critic to Henry who was scanning the titles on gramophone records.

The Ninth was played. The wife came in once or twice while this was being performed by the London Philharmonic Orchestra conducted by Sir Thomas Beecham, but she went out again as quickly as she came in. Patrick sat through the whole of Beethoven's symphony in deepest boredom. He might have been able to appreciate the sublime melody of the great musician had he not on his mind this infernal problem of how to live.

"Listen to that, listen to that," Henry was gesticulating with his hand, raising it up and down like a conductor and humming to himself part of the melody.

169

"Music is the greatest of the arts," he said contentedly. "Think of the thought, the passion of that work."

Somebody was at the door. It was Jane De Vine. Patrick groaned in his heart: he knew now that he would have acres of concertos to walk over led by the fingers of Jane on one of the grand pianos. He hadn't come to hear music. He had come to deal in the stuff of existence. He did not understand the way of wealth. He did not know that a man must not say that he is interested in money. It must always be something else, art of music or religion. Why could he not keep that truth in his mind?

Jane had come to give a run over one of her pieces which she was playing at the Gaiety Theatre on the following Sunday evening. She said so. They all sat more firmly in their seats, the sherry was poured, the piano was played. Mrs. De Vine came in during the piano playing. Another visitor also arrived. The night was looking in from the garden and the trees; the rosebushes became terrifying spectres in the imagination. Mrs. De Vine drew the blinds.

So heavy was his torture becoming that when the drink went around again Patrick took a large tumbler of whiskey instead of the sherry. Then he started to talk. "Music is the least of the arts. There is no thought in music, less even than in painting: its appeal is to the emotions."

Displeasure was written on all faces except the face of the hostess. However, they did not appear surprised: they appeared as if they had expected such an outburst. All these men and women, being men and women of the world, knew what the other man was thinking even when he tried hardest to conceal his thought.

To know what the other was thinking was the secret of business. Any fool can probe his own thoughts. Like a good player who glances once at his own hand of cards and devotes all the rest of his thought and time to the unseen hands of the other players! Life is as simple as a game of poker.

Dr. Cotch came in. He was a man easy to insult too, like his wife in that respect. Not very intelligent looking. He didn't need to be. Jane was still strumming at the piano.

"All the ministers are coming," the doctor whispered to Mrs. De Vine. Patrick drank another whiskey. He was half-drunk now.

"There's no real interest in art in this city," he shouted: "not a bit of real interest."

170

How innocent of him! His very protest was a presupposition that there might possibly be some genuine interest. The only people interested in art are the artists. The artist's or the poet's only real customer is the poet.

The people in the room were angry, not a sincere anger, but an anger that however insincere carried with it all the disadvantages for the one who provoked it.

He could not be a true artist. No man who was a true artist would say such a thing as that. That was a boring remark for any man, not to mention a poet, to make. Glances were turned on him that were the glances of shocked pietism, the voteens who would go to hell without sin.

"I think I'll go," he said at last, "if I'm to catch a bus."

Nobody protested or suggested that he should stay longer. Mrs. De Vine looked at him a little sadly and regretted, or seemed to regret, not being able to help him. She showed him to the door. At the door he said a few remaining remarks and then was gone.

It was like summer night in the country, as he walked along the shady street, he reflected on the De Vines. Henry De Vine was very bitterly patriotic and anti-almost all the things Patrick believed in. He was jealous. Jealous of poets, jealous of everything that had in it the secret of happiness. Patrick had met this type before: they were a dangerous breed, in constant need of being placated. Actors, performers of music and other non-creative workers in the artistic world were praised by him. He also seemed to have a fine capacity for praising all the most contemptible versifiers—— by this bringing Patrick down several pegs. Even though Patrick understood the peculiarly unhappy type of mind that was behind it all, yet it made him uncomfortable and annoyed. If he could only get the flesh of life upon the skeleton of this family's history it would please him immensely. Already something very like the truth was taking shape in his imagination. When he got home he would write it down.

It was useless, absolutely useless hoping for anything from these people. Henry De Vine would see him damned first. But you never know. There was always the chance. Patrick hoped and hope is the greatest of tortures.

Tragedy is life poised on hope, wobbling from one side to the other.

Watching this artistic family with all the accoutrements of

fashionable society upon them Patrick did not wonder that the glare and blare was designed to shut out their squalid past, The slime-stuck peasant unconscious of cities, of cultures, of everything but the power of money, had come to town. Money was everything—— almost.

CHAPTER 7

The Church of Adam and Eve was crowded with unemployed men. It was chiefly for these men that the mid-day Mass was said. Standing amongst these men Patrick's egotism lost some of its edge. He had come to pray for success in the interview, and looking around him at these devout men, and thinking how much he had to thank God for, by comparison with their lot he felt that he was competing for the friendship of God with men who were at a disadvantage. It was like taking another man's rations. Or has God limitless bounty to confer? Do prayers count at all? Of course they count but not as a man expects.

The Bishop and Father Raspoon and all the priests of the church saw no difference between men like these whose apprehensions of the future stretched so short a distance, who were unburdened with a vocation. The poet, the artist, has to be an egotist, has to appear uncharitable—— that he may achieve his destiny.

But the church seeing the souls of men all of like importance could not distinguish the poet from the ordinary man and she was never the patron of the artist.

Patrick was glad when the Mass was nearly over. He did not wait for the end as he had a few things to do before going for the interview at half-past three.

Waiting in a narrow passageway while other men and women were being interviewed Patrick's well-planned attack was losing strategic shape. Perhaps this was the reason men were kept waiting—— so that they arrive on the scene of battle in their very worst spirits. Patrick was the last to be interviewed.

Before coming for the interview he had got several rules which were valuable. First: when he went into the room where the Board sat he was to stand clear of the door before taking his seat. To stand in such a position that the door being opened by someone would bang against him would be a bad sign of his manoeuvreability in an office. Second: He was not to leave his hat on the desk or table in front of him but on the floor beside him. Third: he should not put his hands or elbows on the table but on his knees. This would indicate Jesuit training. Fourth: he was to sit up straight in his chair leaning over towards the Board ever so slightly as occasion demanded. Finally: he must speak in a low voice and always when any of the Board was inclined to go off into subjects which were out of his depth, to interrupt him with an intimate man-to-man or rather pupil to schoolteacher question such as—— "But, sir, don't you rather agree that...."

Patrick had it all off. Putting it into practice was another matter.

For several days he had been seeking information as to who would likely be on the interviewing Board. He had got a list of names of well-known people—— one or other of whom, he was told—— would be sure to know him.

Taking one eyeful of the Board sitting behind the table he immediately marvelled how in so small a city a Board could be got together that looked as foreign as that Board looked to him. He did not recognise a single man or woman—— though naturally all of them must have been of some eminence to be there.

The chairman was a woman, a grey-haired woman of sixty, a literary, artistic type of female. She was all smiles as he entered. All the Board, for that matter, were all smiles and Patrick going in with a determined mind found himself more or less, so to speak, inclined to fall forward for want of resistance.

In all there were five members at the table, two of them being women. The other woman was a young girl, pretty, if a little stout who was—— Patrick gathered from internal conversation—— a young scientist. He found it amusing to see grey-headed savants defer to this interesting female and it convinced him that the standard of judgment in academic circles is a fraudulent standard.

How, thought he, could there be any soundness in such scholarship where a girl who, as a blind man could see, was nothing more than a delightful young woman with thoughts only of love—— or of marriage - in her head being deferred - to by old men. In the shallower reaches of art and music Patrick had observed the same thing, and he knew it was the sign of decadence.

They had been discussing some question of higher physics when Patrick came in and now when he was seated and trying to remember how to look like a Jesuit boy with his palms on his knees they referred back to some knotty point. The young girl was explaining. One of the men, a man of about sixty was speaking to her. The chairman was speaking to Patrick. Nothing of the kind of talk he would have expected of an interviewer; rather it was nice gossipy talk about Patrick's own subject.

"...I'd say Eliot is more like....that."

"Eliot is exciting," Patrick replied, "but there is something decadent about his work. The effect of Eliot—— and of Joyce too—— is that they destroy ideals and not illusions. The difference between a great artist and one who is decadent is that the great artist leaves more in the world than he found, the decadent less. Eliot and Joyce and their school lead us away from the ideal towards utter emptiness and futility. They are the spenders of the spiritual patrimony which great men such as Shakespeare, Dante and Goethe have created. The spending of a fortune is usually more interesting than the slow building up of one, and as a result these decadent poets excite their time, like all spenders and achieve tremendous reputations—— which time deals savagely with. The fact is...."

"... and effect of a curve like this...."

Patrick realised at this point that another learned discussion on science was taking place at the other end of the table. He stopped talking. The others stopped talking too. Now he was being interviewed.

"Have you any experience of this sort of work?"

"I have experience of everything," Patrick replied to the round-faced man who had put the question. "There is really nothing in these things. The people in possession want to make out that what they possess is some sort of esoteric cult beyond the reach of plain man. The politicians do it though we know that to be a politician a man need have no education, no morals, no nothing. The scientists do it, the newspapermen do it. I could run this country: I could run any country. Because what I say is funny, it is funny because it is ridiculously true. And then...."

On and on Patrick ran, from one event to the other, from one theme to another. He knew that he must stop talking but he could not. He was on the run trying to catch up with himself. He had his elbow on the edge of the table. He scratched his head; he shifted his seat. Worst of all, he was falling in love with the young woman student of higher physics. He was capable of being in love with more than one woman, as indeed most men are.

The interview came to an end quicker than he had expected.

He had done most of the talking. He had kept no apparent fund of reserve, that hidden power, or illusion of hidden power, which impresses most. O God! O God! he cried to himself when he was out on the street, after all my planning I made a fool of myself. I talked and I talked instead of letting the others do the talking. He felt exactly as he used to feel after being at a party in the country in his boyhood where he had been tempted to sing and entertain the company and came out of it completely washed up, empty. His nerves tortured him.

He knew that he would not get the job, Every fault that he had ever made before he now made again. He couldn't hold himself in. He gave all out. There was no enigma to intrigue his hearers.

No job! Still, he had a chance of that job. A man never knew. The chairman he did not like. She was too much of the public woman engaged in masculine avocation who feels a sense of her inferiority.

He did not see Margaret that day. He went home and tried to write some verse about her—— to her.

> *You thought how easily might have been lost*
> *All that was me, the verse waiting to be written,*
> *My whole life, and you were conscience-smitten*
> *Wondering whose soul would bear the cost.*

He looked at the verse and a superstitious dread took hold of him: it was dangerous to write down one's fears, one's self-pity, lest in the end it might all come true.

CHAPTER 8

During the evening he had a visit from Robert Hinny: he had come to hear how Patrick fared at the interview. Patrick told him.

"Well, what do you think? How do you think I did?" Patrick asked.

"I was talking to one of the members of the Board—— Lucia Wose—— and she said they were terribly pleased with you altogether. Terribly pleased indeed."

"You think I'll get it?"

"I wouldn't like to be too sure: these jobs go queer."

"Did you know that girl was going to be on the committee, Robert?"

"Well, I think everyone knew who was going to be on it. It was more or less public who would be on it, wasn't it?"

Public! thought Patrick. For three days he had been trying to find out who might possibly be on the interviewing Board and not a man nor woman of his many acquaintances were able to give him a hint. Now when the interview was over everyone knew. It was the same way in everything else. Once when for three months he had endured in silence and cured himself of a whitlow on his little finger, no one during all those weeks was able to tell what his complaint was. Just when he was better, everyone he met seemed to have had a whitlow at one time or another and could tell him all about its correct treatment. We learn everything too late. It seems that men are incapable of hearing—— or if hearing, incapable of understanding—— anything they themselves have not experienced.

"If everyone knew who was to be on the Board then I haven't an earthly chance."

"Everyone has his own trouble, Patrick. This evening Maureen and I were going out and she.... You are not listening to me."

He was right. Patrick was not listening. He was not interested in his visitor's troubles. Robert had come to unload on him some of his domestic difficulties, and to tell Patrick how unhappy he and his wife were. They had everything that money could buy, yet they had not happiness. They were bored. Beyond the superficial interests of golf and cards and visiting, their lives were empty. Robert tried to tell all this to Patrick and Patrick listened in a desultory manner, sometimes getting up to stare disconsolately out the window, or to interrupt with a passionately earnest: "Shocking pity I didn't know in time." Then awakening to the other's story, "What's that?"

Robert left. Patrick started to write again but was too miserable to create. Two forces were wrestling for possession of his soul—the muse and a woman. Poets should be celibates. There should be a place for them where they need not obey the rules of normal life. But again, Patrick did not agree with that theory at all; he believed that the poet was an abnormally normal man and that the fault was in a society created by the uncreative.

If he didn't get the job there was not the slightest hope of his getting married, And he had so dearly wished that he might be able to get married, to take a flat and settle down. There was still hope. He was afraid of the word "hope,"the cruellest world inthe dictionary. He wrote:

O God above
Must I forever live in dreams of love?
Must I forever see as in a glass
The loveliness of life before me pass
Like Margaret, Clare or sunlight on the grass?

Down the town that evening a dilettante friend who wanted someone to whom he could talk literary talk invited Patrick into the fashionably underground bar known as the Buttery.

The bar was crowded with race-goers, jockeys, trainers and owners. Among these Patrick noticed two of the young nieces of Peter De Vine, and on scanning the smoky corners of the bar he saw Dr. Cotch and his wife and the scientist girl, Lucy Wose, who had been on the interviewing Board. If only he had thought of spending his few spare shillings in this place instead of among the poetasters in the other pub he would have had a good chance. All ifs, ifs, ifs. Accursed ifs.

Beside him two men and a woman, somewhat tipsy, were talking. One of them was an excise man who knew something about the financial affairs of the De Vines.

"Do you know how much income and supertax Peter paid last

year?" he asked.

"I'd say a couple of thousand."

"Couple of thousand your hat! Ninety thousand pounds!"

"Really?"

"Really."

The information-giver sipped his drink and looked proud to be able to impart such startling information. The trio went on to discuss the different interests of the De Vines and Patrick was astonished to learn that this family and all its connections owned the newspaper on whose staff Patrick had sought and re-sought employment, and for which he had tried to get the influence of the Bishop and of Father Raspoon. They also had a controlling interest in every one of the firms which Patrick had hoped to break into at one time or another. They owned Plastics, every bit of it.

Patrick was shocked.

As far as he could gather, Father Raspoon was the diplomatic genius behind the money—— he and the Bishop in a more remote dignified way, decided who deserved to have the right to marry and bring up children—— in other words, to get a job. Father Raspoon, they believed was a touchy man, never forgave an injury or an insult. There was nobody he did not know.

So that was it. Patrick thought again. He saw that a man like Father Raspoon became the father of a family vicariously. He helped a relation to get a job and saw him married and bringing up children. Then he arranged another job for some other cousin or neice, and so on and so on.

Patrick listened to this conversation, ignoring the literary interruptions of his companion.

Among the company present in that bar, drinking with the De Vine group were many men whom Patrick had long looked upon as shadowy fellows, like spies or crooks of some kind. They were well-dressed young men who seemed to have no need to go to work. They paraded the social streets and social parlours and they knew everyone that was worth knowing. Patrick saw them on the streets and sometimes he heard of them being present at literary and artistic functions. They knew all the prettiest, wealthiest women and with these they were a great success because, not being poets, they were able to act as a poet is supposed to act.

Don Juans! From where did they derive their incomes? Patrick would like to have known but then finding out such gossip took

179

up so much of a man's time. Making a success of living is a whole-time job and the man who indulges in it has no time for other altruistic artistic pursuits.

It would pay, Patrick realised, to suffer these men and their ways, for they knew the way the wheels of society went round. He would not kow-tow, he would not stoop to such company. He would carry his integrity of mind, though it prove a heavy cross, to the end.

In the bar a woman, very blonde and very drunk came over to Patrick and taking out a comb started to comb his hair. He let her. When she tried to kiss him he put his hand on his forehead and pushed her aside.

"Isn't he sweet?" said she. "Darling, kiss me."

"Go away, you bitch," he said.

"You are a fool," said his companion, "a crass fool."

"Why?" Patrick asked in wonder.

"That one is a first cousin of Father Raspoon. She is terrifically rich and has as much influence as anyone in the city. A shocking man, Kavanagh, you are."

"How was I to know who she was? and even if I did know I'm damned if I'd let her kiss me. Ugly-looking, low-looking creature."

"Two more of those, waiter!"

They drank.

As he feared and expected, Patrick did not get the appointment in Plastics. A young girl had been appointed, he learned. That was that. All his hopes were shattered. Meeting a friend on the street he expressed his despair to him:

"I have no chance in this city," he said, "I'll die in a ditch if I stay here. Nothing surer than that."

"What you ought to do," advised the other, "is what every wise man does——" He sipped his drink, "what every wise man does."

"What does every wise man do?"

"Wise writer, I mean."

"Well, what does the wise writer do?"

"Marries a rich woman". The man settled down to explain. He faced Patrick. "You get a woman with money and you can have all the other things—— young women, as many as you want. Look at them all here," he gesticulated. "There, there are dozens of them. All a man needs is money. If I were you," he lowered his voice, "I'd go for someone like for instance Jane De Vine. It's my ex-

180

perience that the higher up you go the easier it is to get them". He paused.

"Why don't you do that?" asked Patrick.

"I'm going to do it. I was out with a fellow the other night at a party in Howth and I met there a few that would suit. I...."

The man went on explaining. He talked till closing time all about wealthy women and how to get them. The whole thing seemed slightly mad, screwy, fantastic. But society, as Patrick was learning to understand, was based on a lunatic idea. Madness had become the norm of these people's ideal and a rational man like Patrick was considered the lunatic.

Lying in bed awake Patrick thought over the man's advice. To marry a rich woman was not the silliest thing a writer could do. Shaw had done it and many others. But what a price they had to pay! And the upshot of it all was that having compromised on their deepest beliefs and feelings they had not succeeded as artists. It does not pay a man to compromise. Patrick pledged himself before falling asleep that whatever might happen he would not compromise the world. He would either marry the woman of his choice or he would marry none. He would always strive towards his ideal though he were to die of despair.

In the morning he wrote, but he found it hard to write without the security of at least one whole week as a grip for his mind. Yet he tried. He spent the first half of the day writing verses and when tired out turned to the prose sketch for which the editor of the *Irish Times* had already paid him.

He thought how interesting it would be to write about the De Vines. He would write a story of their hidden lives if only he had some facts to go on. He had no facts. The De Vines were an enigma. They owned the city. The Bishop, who disclaimed any pull or power was the equivalent of a king in the country. Father Raspoon could have got him any job he wished. If only he had been nicer to Mrs. De Vine!

For a moment he breathed in the feelings of the middle-class crowd who frequented the Buttery Bar and who played golf and Bridge and went to parties—— and breathing that feeling he partook of a new food of experience. He would write about the tragedy of those who had all that money but could not buy with it all the marvellous things of life, things he himself had. A purpose in life. He had a purpose in life. He had a struggle. Suddenly it occurred to him that he might easily get rich and in doing so lose that sense of purpose, that missionary urge. And the thought made him wonder if he really wanted to succeed in the ways of the world.

But then there was Margaret. Without money he could not have her. He met her by arrangement that evening and they went for a walk through the park.

"Have you any news?"

That meant had he any news of a job. Patrick had hopes. "Wonderful chance of a job coming next week, Margaret, I'm going to be rich, do you know that?"

She laughed and bantered him. He was always going to be rich next week.

"You are shockingly disreputable, Patrick. Look at that tie! and those shoes! And that suit! Get rid of it as soon as you can. If I had it I'd burn it, for it is neither artistically shabby nor respectably smart. You are neither one thing nor the other. And I wish you wouldn't laugh out loud the way you do. You are far too natural. Take shorter steps."

She watched his walk standing a few yards behind him to see how he progressed.

"Well," said he stopping, "How is that?"

"A little better. And straighten your shoulders—— And that's the one was on the committee!" Margaret said referring to an earlier part of the conversation, "I know her cousin well."

"And I bet you know the daughter of Dr. Cotch?"

"Of course I know her. What difference does that make? Don't you know all these people too? The only thing for you to do is to work, work, work. Keep writing and you won't be long poor.

"I do work; I'm working like a savage."

"What are you writing? How many words did you write today?"

"A lot."

"About how many?"

"Oh, I don't know—— how could I know? You see, the worst of it is with you, you measure everything materially. Supposing I wrote a poem that was destined to be immortal according to your way of judging, it would be worth very little. Don't you see?"

"That's your way of saying you did nothing, Patrick. I am sure that the poets who wrote immortal poems wrote a lot of words before they gor to the immortal one."

182

Patrick was amazed at her acuteness. She was just like his mother in nearly everything. She could tell what he was thinking: she could know what he was doing when she was miles away from him. He knew it. Many a time when he sat idly about he could feel her presence and her chastisement. She was great, she was wonderful, and he was the laziest man alive in the country. Once when he told her he would willingly die for her she laughed and said that he wouldn't even give up the cigarettes for her. He smoked far too much.

Did he desire her physically? He did, but that physical desire was a small part of his desire—— and of hers. There are two kinds of women: those who evoke physical desire alone and those who call out the whole man, body and mind. These are the women whom men should marry. Margaret was one of these. Not that she was without passion. Far from it. She awakened in him fires of excitement much more intense than any woman had every done before, but so great was her general appeal that he scarcely was conscious of the animal instinct.

Fools write about love—— and talk about love—— and they knew nothing about love. Men who base everything upon sex are called psychologists, but they are shallow men—— for the physical act is not the miracle of creation, nor even the cause of it—— only the Divine Creator.

In idealism is truth. Materialism is only one side of the material.

He asked Margaret to come into a restaurant to have some coffee. She refused.

"You're ashamed to be seen with me," he said.

She turned up her eyes in naïve agony. They were standing outside the restaurant.

"Listen! Don't make a show of me here," she pleaded.

"Ah, come on in."

"I said I wouldn't go in and isn't that enough?"

"I never met anyone like you."

She made to go off. He followed her. She moved faster. He caught up with her and without speaking was walking by her side for fifty yards.

"My goodness me," she cried, "Didn't I tell you to go and work and that nothing would please me more. Didn't I tell you that?"

"I know, I know, but you mightn't have run off like that."

"What do you want me to do now? Will you go home please?"

"All right, all right, but...."

She was gone round the corner towards her house and he was left there—— dissatisfied.

She didn't love him, he said to himself. If she loved him she wouldn't have run off like that. He thought back and remembered all the times when she showed the same fickleness. Before going home he would go down to the G.P.O. and write her a letter explaining with a writer's precision exactly what he wanted to explain. He bought a Letter-Card and crooking his arm around it so as not to let a certain man who knew him catch a glimpse of what he was writing, wrote:

"My dearest Margaret, It was very mean of you to run off this evening. You should not do a thing like that—— especially to a writer. My temptation is to run after you if you run away and that lacks dignity. I have come to the conclusion that you do not really like me...."

He read over what he had written and decided that it would be better not to write. It was not through writing that he met her in the first place so why?

He tore up the Letter-Card and took the stamp part and put it in his pocket. He thought a long while at the door of the post office. Should he go back and try another letter? A man who did nothing could never go wrong but he got nowhere. He bought a second Letter-Card and wrote:

"My dear Margaret, I wonder would you meet me tomorrow in the cafe? Come if you can but if you cannot come it will be alright. If you cannot come tomorrow I'll be in the same cafe the next day at the same time. The day after that I'll be having lunch in the Green Restaurant. So if you want to see me you'll know. I want to make it clear to you that you are free to do as you please. I do not wish to exercise any influence over you. You know I do not—— and never did—— believe in the ludicrous idea of love. I just like you.
Love Patrick.

He closed the Letter-Card and wrote the address in large handwriting. He remembered that he once had been interested in a girl and had written to her an idiotic letter in very small script—— and that was the unluckiest letter he had ever written. He was fairly satisfied with this letter. There was nothing in it that compromised him and he had left the issue open so that if she did not come it would not mean a rebuff. He held it on the edge of the posting box for about ten seconds before dropping it in. Collecting all his courage he relaxed his fingers and—— for good or ill—— the letter was posted.

There was no hope. Three weeks later Margaret told him she had the opportunity of marrying someone else and Patrick agreed that this was the right thing for her to do. She must not sacrifice herself to him. The same fate that was destroying him would eventually also destroy her. He would carry on. Tearfully she agreed.

EPILOGUE : Peter Kavanagh

It would be pointless to continue to write in detail of Patrick's pilgrimage through Dublin during the following twenty-five years. Relentlessly the pattern already established repeated itself. Occasionally new characters appeared but that was all. The cycle began with immense hope and ended inevitably with defeat. Patrick wrote:

When I review this long and terrible period of folly I find it rather difficult to reconstruct the scene. That is the way with unpleasant things, at least with me. You may have been hungry for a couple of hours but when you are fed you have forgotten the whole thing.

I am not going to speak of the war years which, I suppose were bad enough. What I am speaking of are the years from about 1947 to 1956.

I am speaking of this experience, I must emphasise, because it illuminates something of the poetic view and what happens to some kinds of men is for the benefit of everyman. It is a fact that I starved. It is a fact that I would have died of starvation had it not been for the charity of some friends. I can state that on many Christmas days, those days when we feel that things are different, I sat in my frowsy flat with nothing to eat and uninvited by anyone. These are the simple facts which I here put on the record.

If I compare my state with that of Dante it is for no purpose of vanity, yet somehow I cannot help feeling a fellow-feeling.

Of course we have no right to expect friendship or charity. If a man chooses to be a poet he must expect what comes of that choice.

The Bishop here involved with Patrick was John Charles McQuaid, Archbishop of Dublin. It is easy to forget that John Charles was under no obligation to help Patrick in any way——

Patrick was not a politician, a clergyman or a relative. Had the Archbishop any real power? The position certainly carried immense prestige and it is unlikely that any employer would refuse someone recommended by so prestigous a source. John Charles did not want to exercise that power he had on behalf of Patrick. There are many reasons we can imagine but one especially is worth noting. The Archbishop was in awe of his position. He had been pushed into the job by De Valera in token of the help John Charles had given in helping to write the Irish Constitution. He was a pious man who said his prayers and gave charity to the needy. He had no concept of the larger view of Christianity as illustrated by Renaissance prelates.

Nor, of course, had he any concept of poetry except for what he had heard of the dissolute lives of those who wrote the stuff. It is unlikely that he viewed Patrick any differently from the masses of Dublin poetasters. How could he tell, and if he were able to make the distinction, should he treat Patrick as a special case? After all, Patrick had but one soul and there were thousands of needy people in his diocese each with a similar soul. It was only right, he must have thought, to give evenly of his charity.

He did not trust Patrick. No doubt he had his reasons. Patrick recognized the distrust and could hardly have concealed his resentment. Nor should one expect the Archbishop to give something for nothing—— excluding charity. He saw no sign that Patrick was prepared to give anything in return for his patronage should he receive it. Patrick could be a great source of information on the literary underground yet he was not gossipy nor did he come forward with anything that might be called worthwhile intelligence. John Charles had even tried him out on this angle and got no return. There was a statue of Christ the King by Andrew O'Connor which his family were pressing to have erected in Dun Laoghaire in fulfilment of a contract. John Charles saw heresy in the position of the hands of the Christus. He would like to see the statue dumped in Scotsman's Bay but was concerned about the public's reaction. So he told Patrick it had so been disposed of, hoping Patrick would spread the story. Patrick told me in confidence but no one else. He took the story as true and would not betray a confidence. Twenty years later the statue was discovered in the back garden of the lawyer who acted for the Archbishop. Patrick was infuriated when he saw that John Charles had tried to make a fool out of him. He himself would never tell a lie and he could not imagine that the Archbishop would tell one either. Only with great difficulty was I able to persuade Patrick not to write a scorching letter to his benefactor. I regret my interference.

But in spite of his defects, John Charles was the only one in Dublin who came close to being a friend. He gave Patrick the odd five pound note and on several occasions rescued him from eviction by paying the rent past due. And when Patrick fell ill he did not hesitate to visit him at the hospital and guarantee him a private room in the Mater Hospital should he ever suffer a relapse. Who else in Dublin made anything comparable to that kind of offer? Who else could compare with him? He did not do the large thing—— that was not in his character—— but on the level of charity he was exceptional.

I lived with Patrick during many of those bleak years and while I have no great enthusiasm to recall them, a few memories force themselves on me.

First, the large, empty and freezing flat at 62 Pembroke Road where we lived. The wind blew through the rooms from the holes in the uncalked window frames. There were marble fireplaces in each room but we could not afford fuel for the fires. Patrick lived in one large room towards the front, I in another. The rooms were separated by folding doors.

I am toiling with my book on the Irish Theatre. He is inside tapping on his typewriter. The typewriter stops and the folding doors open. Patrick comes in with a sheet of paper in his hand. He is slightly diffident because of the intrusion. "I have something here I'd like to read you," he says. I listen and give my opinion. "You're right, you're right! I see that. I'll re-write it later."

The conversation turns to some topic of local interest. We make a cup of tea. The conversation continues: it builds up until we both explode into the wildest laughter. Never, never, shall I laugh like that again.

Then off we go for a walk into town. We are out on the street when Patrick stops. "Are you sure you have turned off the gas?" He goes back to check. A more cautious or reliable man I have never known since. If I arrange to meet him at a certain hour he will be there to the second. He never fails.

In those days Patrick never drank. He was strictly a tea-shop devotee. Only when cancer began moving-in did he resort to the drink. There may be some connection.

Patrick at this time was also the subject of almost daily controversy in *The Irish Times*. Whatever he wrote caused massive response from readers. An uninformed outsider might be excused for imagining that Patrick was making a fortune. Patrick received no payment for the controversy and had to be satisfied with the guinea he received from the original essay.

Poverty — here is Patrick's definition:

It consists in a belief in the power of money. Of course I know that money is power but this belief is something else. St. Francis was said to have chosen poverty. But I deny that a man can choose poverty. If chosen, it is not the same thing. St. Francis had plenty of money and he threw it away and was free. Real poverty is never free.

Although I was sharing my miserable income with Patrick I was not truly in poverty. I was somewhat in the position of St. Francis, I was giving my money away freely. It was voluntary poverty. Then came my Ph.D. in 1946 and I was a free man — free from the bondage of teaching in a National School under inhuman conditions. I left for America and within a year I was Professor at Loyola University in Chicago. Patrick was delighted with my achievement and planned to follow me. I still have the official papers that I signed for him.

Just at that moment Macmillans gave Patrick an advance on a book he promised to write for them. It was too large to refuse and too small to liberate. It held him suspended; he cancelled his idea of going to America. I continued to help him financially and now and then bailed him out of difficult positions. We kept up a close correspondence which has since been published. I also returned to Ireland almost every year.

When I came back in 1952 Patrick's wheel of fortune had once more arrived at that black mark which threatened despair. Not only was he in poverty but even the outlets for his journalism had dried up. He was isolated. He at first suggested, then insisted, that I help him start his own newspaper. I had a few thousand dollars in savings and I decided to spend it on rescuing Patrick from this frustrating position. So began *Kavanagh's Weekly*. When my money ran out we would close down. That was the plan. We closed with the thirteenth issue. With the exception of one or two pieces we wrote everything ourselves. We received no help. Much malicious advice was freely tendered. The story of *Kavanagh's Weekly* is so well known that it need not be retold here.

After the *Weekly* folded I returned to America to recover my financial stability. Patrick moved temporarily to London. Dublin's bitterness, suppressed for thirteen weeks, boiled over. It found expression in a "Profile" of Patrick which appeared in a weekly magazine called *The Leader*. What was written was clearly defamatory of both Patrick and myself. Patrick decided to sue for libel and I cheered him on. Next followed the notorious law case which a Dublin jury decided against Patrick and, need I say, against the evidence. Had they found for Patrick and given him damages contemptuous that would have been the end of it. No appeal could possibly succeed. But the jury, reflecting the mood of Dublin, chose to be vindictive. The decision was so absurd that there had to be an appeal to the Supreme Court. After an appeal that went on in the Supreme Court for ten days we won the right to a new trial.

The hatred engendered by Patrick was exceptional even for Dublin. He was willing to settle the libel action before going to trial for a hundred pounds but the opposition would not consider it. Patrick had to be destroyed. And so the case went to trial with Patrick kept in the box under the most villainous cross-examination for ten days against all ethics of the legal profession. Towards the end Patrick was in such a nervous condition that he couldn't swallow. I warned him that he must let go, break down if necessary, or he would be in jeopardy. Eventually he broke down and the trial ended. Why was Patrick so hated? Here is Patrick's analysis of the phenomonon.

> *A poet, or any man, speaking from his Helicon of authority has no audience: he is delivering a statement of the gods. Anyone that likes may listen.*
> *It is this authority that maddens mean people, and one of the main reasons it maddens them is that it is so funny. The god delivering judgment is always in the mood for uproarious laughter. This is an unforgivable quality. The ordinary man trying to be somebody must have Art—— art of film, art of theatre, art of acting. The poetic man doesn't give a damn about art. Laughter is one of the cruellest reasons why people leave old Skibbereen.*
> *A fact.*

191

The majority of men will never forgive you for being comic about the dull little things by which they try to beat the artistic rap. Art is a very solemn world, not a laugh in an acre of it.

Of course I am not talking about ordinary coarse laughter; I am talking of the gaiety of authority and truth.

There is nothing as funny as a true poet. This is one of the tests.

Why the non-poetic thing is unfunny and deadly dull and solemn is because of its awful unseriousness. The poet's comic spirit is real seriousness, the seriousness that will die for its ideal in the last ditch.

The solemn art humbug will bale out at the first hint of trouble.

It took me a long time to learn all this and it is part of my real autobiography. The majority of physical things that happen to a man are of no importance; the self is only interesting as an illustration.

Just before the law case opened I moved to London where I established myself as Public Relations Officer for a large engineering company. Patrick was delighted with my success and tried to boast a bit about it but without effect. Only misfortune is news.

Then suddenly as we were awaiting the result of the Surpeme Court decision disaster struck. Patrick became ill. He had suspected something wrong a year before and visited Baggot Street Hospital. They told him he was in excellent health and suffering from a tense imagination. Now the diagnosis was possible cancer. The doctors wouldn't know until they opened him up. All decisions now devolved on me. It was a heavy responsibility. I gave instructions to operate. It was discovered that Patrick had indeed cancer of the lung. It had to be removed. No one thought he would survive.

But Patrick did not die. His powerful constitution and athletic development were important assets. In addition there was his will to live. For a long time he had postponed certain projects and he was now determined if at all possible to complete them.

When he was on the road to recovery I bought him a new suit so that he could look "respectable" when he was leaving hospital. He always had a desire to look like a prosperous businessman. Buying the suit evoked in me a feeling of pathos, almost of tragedy. Here was I buying a suit for someone I admired: it was as if I were buying it for a child. As it turned out he was unable to wear the suit; it was too heavy for him to carry in his weakened condition.

We were both wondering where he could go to recuperate when a "friend" of his made an enthusiastic offer to put him up in a nearby Nursing Home and pay his expenses. Meanwhile he could stay at the Hibernian Hotel at the "friend's" expense. As might have been forecast the "friend" disappeared and I had to foot the bill. Patrick spent a month recuperating in Longford with his sisters, then came back to Dublin.

He was now confronted with a number of difficult problems—the difficulty of climbing steps with only one lung, speaking with damaged vocal cords and most of all, how to avoid getting a cold since pneumonia would be instantly fatal. I omit altogether his chronic condition of having no income whatever.

Then John Costello, opposing council in the law case came to his aid. Costello had been Prime Minister for a time and was now seeking re-election. Patrick was emerging from a polling booth when he ran into Costello. They shook hands and Costello apologetically remarked that he hoped Patrick did not hold any resentment against him over the law case. "Resentment?", said Patrick, "I just voted for you". Costello at once went to Tierney, head of UCD and arranged a sinecure for Patrick— he was to be paid three hundred pounds a year and would be expected to give a series of public lectures on poetry. No big deal but enough to save Patrick from total dependence on me.

No one envied Patrick the sinecure— it was not expected that he would live long enough to enjoy it. Once more he proved his ill-wishers wrong. He lived for a further twelve years.

In addition to the sinecure Patrick found himself a job writing a weekly column for *The Farmer's Journal.*

At this point I consulted with Patrick's physician who gave me some startling advice. Patrick, he said, was cured of the cancer and would survive. He could not give a similar assurance about my survival. Because of all the tension I was in considerable danger. He advised strongly that I cut loose from that tension. I had no choice but agree. So I returned to America. The doctor proved to be right for within a period of three months I was in hospital twice and now it was Patrick who was doing the worrying. However, I recovered and Patrick was over to visit me the following year.

This was Patrick's first visit to New York. He fell in love with the place and stayed almost five months. The enthusiasm he received from New Yorkers made Patrick forget his own admonitions to me to have nothing whatever to do with anyone Irish or representing Ireland abroad. When St. Patrick's Day came there he was on the parade stand with the Mayor of Dublin. Patrick extended his hand in friendship. The Mayor put on his most offensive scowl and turned his back. A similar reception awaited Patrick when he called on the Irish delegation to the United Nations.

I myself must admit responsibility by indirection for an even worse insult given him. He was interested in earning some money so I had two of my friends arrange that he give a lecture on poetry to Marymount College—— a Catholic college that considered itself chic, Catholic and very Irish. When Patrick showed up huffing and puffing with his one lung they turned him away saying he was drunk and unfit to appear before their polite audience. The sister in charge called me up to explain. I told her how I regarded her behaviour. They paid him his fee of a hundred dollars. Patrick assuaged his hurt feelings by taking the money next day to Aqueduct where he gambled it on the track. The money, as might be expected, carried no luck with it.

It was also on this trip that he decided to visit Ezra Pound, incarcerated in St. Elizabeth's Lunatic Asylum in Washington D.C. He was disappointed in the meeting—— as I had been some years earlier. Pound was still in his Imagist cocoon and had scarcely moved forward. Patrick found he had little in common with him.

The orderly at the admissions desk had given Patrick the usual forms to fill. Patrick signed: "Patrick Kavanagh, Dublin." The orderly scanned it musingly and added, "England."

"Ireland", Patrick protested.

"It's all the same", said the orderly.

And now, back once more to Ireland——

In a Letter to the magazine *Nimbus* (1956) Patrick advised that he was sending along his Irish environment with the Letter. Here is part of that essay:

"An opportunity to send on this environment occurred recently. I was invited to speak at a debate organized by a British Railways Staff Debating Society. The place was crowded as will be seen from the unmannerly paragraph which I include as a sample of the malice and dislike for the remote unapproachable soul. Cheapen him, "Paddy" him. This element is always looking for a poet who can be trained to be clown. Here is some of my speech:

> *I note that in the promotion sheet of this meeting I am the only one who has a profession attributed to him—— Patrick Kavanagh, Poet. This puts me at a disadvantage: how am I to know that one of the other debaters isn't an ex-heavyweight boxer with a nasty temper? This is a typical Irish kind of bad manners. A large number of people, particularly newspaper illiterates are always trying to imply that the term poet and silly idiot are synonymous. This is an attitude I will only accept from very beautiful women....*
> *As for the Censorship it does not concern the creative writer. The Censorship operates in a lower-middlebrow milieu. The one organization that I would be terrified of getting into power is that which calls itself the Friends of Civil Liberty.... It is my duty to tell you that these people are the enemies of liberty. Liberty is largeness. Liberty is positive. You are not supporting literature by negatively attacking the Censorship: you support it by supporting with cash a writer of talent if you know one. I know that when a test came a couple of years ago when I was fighting a cause before a judge and jury in Dublin there wasn't one of these Friends of Liberty, opponents of the Censorship, complainers about the power of the Catholic Church who didn't work night and day to dishonour, discredit, humiliate, and utterly destroy everything for which the word 'poet' stands.*

This speech did not get into the newspapers. Instead the following paragraph was typical.

> *The billing of Paddy Kavanagh, Poet, as one of the speakers last night at the British Railways Staff Association Debating Society was one of the reasons why we, with many others, went along to the Four Courts' Hotel.*
> *While we more or less fought our way in through a packed house it was a bit disconcerting to meet Mr. Kavanagh fighting his way out, temporarily as it happened. Mr. Kavanagh's speech was not one of his best but the audience loved it.*

And so there you have some of my environment which is not entirely an, envelope of stone,. And you will note too that this must be one of the rare occasions when a man going to the lavatory was news."

Shortly after Patrick came out of hospital and was recuperating on the banks of the Grand Canal, lazing there in the sun, he was reborn. That is what he said. Fate had done its worst. Let the wheel turn as it might. He would pay no heed to it. He no longer cared for what the world offered. He would concentrate on his special mission, the writing of verse, the kingdom of God in poetry. At once he began producing poems of great beauty and intensity. No one was interested in publishing them but what matter. He had defeated death, he had fulfilled his destiny.

He sent me a selection. I was startled and excited. I would publish them. Why not? And so began the Peter Kavanagh Hand Press, my first publication being **Recent Poems**. This collection was later published in England under the title **Come Dance With Kitty Stobling**.

In 1956 he gave his first series of lectures at UCD. I wasn't there but he reported that they were a great success–– an orgy of emotion. He handed the typescript of the lectures to the university for publication but they were turned down as unworthy. With his second series in 1958 he was more experienced and instead of giving them to the University Press he gave them to me. I published them eventually in **November Haggard**. Brilliant lectures.

Now that he had a little money Patrick began making occasional excursions to London. On one of these in 1956 he met David Wright, the English poet, who was then editing the magazine *Nimbus*. Patrick was asked to contribute and later, when Wright started the magazine *X,* he was again invited. It was clear to David Wright that Patrick was not just another Irish writer–– he was the writer, the poet, and at once he began announcing to everyone within earshot that Patrick was "the goods".

London's literary pub at that time was The Plough, near the British Museum. Whenever Patrick visited London he made The Plough his headquarters. It interested him on several levels but primarily because it was the meeting place of several London book publishers. Patrick's major hope at this time was to have his **Collected Poems** published before he died. It was rough going for a long time but Patrick had trained in the slum pubs of Dublin and was equal to the challenge. Several times he was threatened with eviction from the saloon for resting his thrombosis-affected leg on an adjoining chair and constantly he was jeered at because of his inability to climb upstairs to the lavatory. This coarse joke was continued after his death and an indecent plaque was erected outside the saloon commemorating this physical handicap. I tore it down.

Patrick, using his native cunning, took insults as compliments and kept me informed. Meanwhile, he would enjoy the vicarious excitement engendered by the clientele. It was an important centre for him at this time and that was reason enough to endure it.

Eventually Patrick's turn came–– McGibbon & Kee would publish his **Collected Poems** –– they would take a chance on them. Patrick was too ill to do the job of collecting and editing. The **Collected Poems** duly appeared in 1964 and were a great success with reviewers.

McGibbon & Kee, without informing Patrick, sold a thousand sheets of *Collected Poems* to a New York publisher whom he detested, claiming in explanation that they had this right under the terms of the contract. Patrick responded to this shock to his sensibilities by giving me Power of Attorney in the United States with orders to savage the American edition. Already I had taken out copyright on a large segment of the collection and therefore I was on solid legal grounds. Patrick of course never disclosed his action, nor did I. He just kept on talking, kept on drinking, and before long the same publisher issued his **Collected Pruse**. For a joke he called it *pruse,* giving it the affected English pronounciation since he always contended there was no such thing as prose, just good writing.

Patrick had now achieved one of his major objectives. Success came late but it came, and he was intent on enjoying it. Prudence is a virtue only in the young so he threw prudence to the wind and began to live for the moment. Besides having only one lung, he had a bad heart, a damaged liver, a doubtful stomach and thrombosis of the leg. He knew he had not long to live so why should he not act as incautious as he chose. Besides, he knew he had me behind the scenes taking care of the record.

What now was the attitude of his neighbours in Inniskeen? The mood of disregard ended in 1962 after his Television appearance in *Self Portrait.* They saw him take the medium they admired most and dominate it. I was home on the bus from Dundalk with him the day after that telecast. As we got off the bus near our house the bus driver shouted after us "Good man, Paddy! You didn't let us down!" Neither of us replied though we were amazed at this peculiar attitude.

In 1965 Northwestern University near Chicago contributed to Patrick's entertainment by inviting him with several others to attend ceremonies at the university celebrating the centenary of the birth of W.B. Yeats. His expenses were to be paid so he accepted eagerly. I tried to warn Patrick in advance of the low standard of education and of manners of American universities. Patrick assured me he was well fit for the situation. The fact is that he wasn't at all fit for it—— he was insulted and abused beyond all decency. In an interview later he explained:

It takes two to make a row and it also takes two to make an agreement, and there was none of that in the audience. They were antagonistic to my viewpoint, more antagonistic than an Irish audience. Here they were positively wrong. It is complete negation in America. You are never to mention Longfellow, Bret Harte or Vachel Lindsay. No one that's alive.

Even Patrick's sense of humour was lost on his audience. When Padraic Colum, in pain, asked Patrick why he made disparaging remarks about Yeats Patrick replied with one word: "spite". Colum took his answer seriously and mentioned it publicly several times later.

After his tour at Northwestern Patrick stayed with us here in New York for six weeks enjoying the city immensely. New York was his town. "It's about the only place in America," he said, "that's fit for living."

This was his final trip to America.

It is curious how all through Patrick's life those in positions of power and those in the business of literature chose to pretend that Patrick was a wild impulsive fellow. I who knew him best found him to be an ultra-conservative. He was my godfather and even took that obligation seriously.

The truth of course is that these idiotic people only pretended to think Patrick wild and impulsive. It was their response to his cutting morality. They hoped to damn him with a label, the eccentric poet, the shoemaker's son out of his depth. All sorts of ugly stories were invented to discredit him: that he read the newspaper in church, that he was dangerous, that he was anti-Catholic.

Even today further stories are being manufactured.

None of this matters very much, now that his work is published and can be judged free of prejudice. From my point of view in addition to being a poet he was also an intense Catholic, almost a mystic. He himself summed up his philosophy of literature and of life.

> The soul has no trade. It is not the son of a shoemaker, or of a farmer, or of a labourer, or of a slum dweller.
>
> The whole struggle in life is the struggle to overcome the flaws in the soul, and this can only be done by will and by grace. Our success or failure in this life does not depend on whether we have been born in cabins or in castles, the sons of shoemakers or of princes, but on the result of our battle with the Seven Deadly Sins. All great literature from Homer to the present is concerned with these battles and may be described as a commentary on them.

Patrick died in Dublin on 30th November 1967. He was given an exuberant funeral.